MEMORIES OF GRIMSBY

TRUE NORTH BOOKS

DEAN CLOUGH

HALIFAX

WEST YORKSHIRE

HX3 5AX

TEL 01422 344344

THE PUBLISHERS WOULD LIKE TO THANK THE
FOLLOWING COMPANIES FOR SUPPORTING THE
PRODUCTION OF THIS BOOK

MAIN SPONSOR
LINDSEY OIL REFINERY LIMITED

ASSOCIATED COLD STORES & TRANSPORT LIMITED

JAMES BRATTON & COMPANY LIMITED

HARRY CARR LIMITED

CRAY VALLEY - TOTAL

FRESHNEY PLACE SHOPPING CENTRE

GRIMSBY PIPEWORK & ENGINEERING LIMITED

SIMON STORAGE COMPANY LIMITED

SSM COAL LIMITED

JOHN SUTCLIFFE & SON (GRIMSBY) LIMITED

TIOXIDE EUROPE LIMITED

WILKIN CHAPMAN SOLICITORS

First published in Great Britain by True North Books
Dean Clough
Halifax HX3 5AX
1998

ISBN 1 900 463 97 0

Introduction

Welcome to *Memories of Grimsby*, a look back on some of the places, events and people in the town which have shaped our lives over a period of around half a century. The following pages are brought to life by the selection of images from the not-too-distant past, chosen according to their ability to rekindle fond memories of days gone by and show how people used to shop, work and play in the town where they grew up. Modern image reproduction techniques have enabled us to present these pictures in a way rarely seen before. The chosen period covered is one which generally contains events within the memory of a large number of people in Grimsby - this is not a book about crinolines or bowler-hats! Neither is *Memories of Grimsby* a work of local history in the normal sense of the term. It has far more to do with entertainment than serious study, but we hope you will agree it is none the worse for that.

Many local companies and organisations have allowed us to study their archives and include their history - and fascinating reading it makes too. The present-day guardians of the companies concerned are proud of their products, the achievements of their people and the hard work of their forefathers whose efforts created these long established firms. When we began compiling *Memories of Grimsby* several months ago we anticipated that the task would be a pleasurable one, but our expectations were greatly surpassed. The quality of the photographs we have been privileged to use has been superb, and the assistance we have received from the staff at Grimsby's Reference Library made

A view of the Old Market Place, dating from the 1960s

our work very enjoyable. There is much talk in modern times about the regeneration of the local economy, the influx of new industries and the challenge of attracting new enterprise from other regions to Grimsby. And quite right too. We could, however, make the mistake of thinking that the changes are all happening *now,* but the reality is that there have always been major developments going on in the town. 'Change' is relentless and the photographs on the pages in the book serve to remind us of a mere a selection of them. Whatever the view taken on the boundaries which separate 'history', 'nostalgia' and the present time we should all invest a little time occasionally to reflect on the past and the people and events which made our town what it is today.

Memories of Grimsby has been a pleasure to compile, we sincerely hope you enjoy reading it.

Happy memories!

ACKNOWLEDGMENTS

We gratefully acknowledge the assistance given in the preparation of this book by Jayne Ayscough and her family. Thanks also are due to North East Lincolnshire Museums Service and North East Lincolnshire Council Libraries, Local History Collection.

TEXT	PHIL HOLLAND
COVER DESIGN/PHOTOGRAPH COMPILATION	MARK SMITH
DESIGNERS	MANDY WALKER, NICKY BRIGHTON AND CHRISTINE GALE
BUSINESS DEVELOPMENT EDITOR	ANDREW HALES

CONTENTS

Around the town centre

NEL Museums

1930s retailers in Grimsby's Victoria Street used to foster an image of 'quality' and exclusivity for their businesses in this popular and respected part of the town. To the modern reader the sight of this trolley bus gliding down the centre of the street will be unusual. Having just trundled around the corner it would have already passed the open market and the Old Market Place. Its way was now clear to travel past *Halfords* cycle shop and journey right the way through to Cleethorpes. Cycles abound and one or two of them had been left unattended, not that there was too much risk associated with that in 1939. Pedestrianisation and the re-routing of many of our town centre roads has changed the character of this part of Grimsby almost beyond recognition.

Above: The top end of Freeman Street was a hive of activity when this scene was captured in the 1930s. A variety of different forms of transport ranging from bicycles to handcarts and a trolley bus add interest to the scene.

The trolley bus in the centre of this picture looks odd to modern eyes, with the long trolley poles reaching out a crazy angle in order to pick up the electric current from the overhead cables.

The vehicles were quiet and smooth-running and were sorely missed when phased out in favour of petrol and diesel powered transport. This single-decker was one of five similar *Garrett* types purchased by the Corporation in 1926.

Right: This 1950s view of the Old Market Place is certain to rekindle memories among people who shopped, worked or simply passed through this part of town. The Old Corn Exchange building can be seen on the left of the photograph and a sign above the substantial doorway advertises snooker at the *Chantry Billiard Rooms* - 5 full size tables for 'good snooker' between 10 am and 11 pm. The establishment was, of course, closed on Sundays. Just beside the entrance a stylish Riley saloon car is about to drive into the main street. Trolley buses add character and atmosphere to the scene, as does the handcart used for town centre deliveries and left casually outside one of the local shops. Some of the shops featured include well-known names such as L & G Modes, Dainties Ltd, Maltby Coates and the 'shop under the clock.'

Above: This photograph was taken to record the preliminary work on the construction site of the *new* Grimsby Library building. In the foreground is Doughty Road as it appeared in the early years of the 1960s, and a row of wonderfully nostalgic motor cars from the time can be seen parked beneath hoardings promoting popular products of the day. The library itself would be built behind these advertising boards in the weeks and months ahead. On the right another 'modern' building is shown with scaffolding in place. This was to become *Pearl Assurance House* on busy George Street. On the right of the picture are buildings which would find use as a charity shop and cafe in later years. The modern library building is an important facility for *Grimbarians* and one of which they can all be proud. More mature readers will be aware that the *old* library was bombed during the Second World War and that a variety of temporary premises were used until the fine new building was secured. The difficult period in the interim was managed by the hard-working librarian of the day Mr Eddie Trevitt.

Right: Timothy Whites the popular chemist was once known as *Timothy Whites and Taylors* and was later absorbed into the giant Nottingham-based Boots group of companies. This busy Grimsby branch was located on the corner of West St. Mary's Gate. The next shop along was The Chocolate Box, and other businesses along Victoria Street included the Electricity Shop, G W Herbert the shoe retailer and the Savoy cinema.

Above: *A scene dominated by around thirty 1950s and '60s motorcars features the Market Square in Grimsby. The mock-tudor frontage of the pestle and Mortar public house acts as a reference point for us on the right of the picture. On the left the georgian-style substantial property housing R.C Johnson's the chemist at 28 and 29 Market Square can be seen and most of the shops have their sun-shades extended to protect the goods in their windows. Further along the street were the businesses operated by the British School of Motoring and Maypole Dairies.*

Left: *A stock-taking sale was taking place at Guy and Smith's store on the left of the photo-graph when this 1960s scene was captured. Perhaps some of the ladies walking along Victoria Street in their short-sleeved summer dresses were attracted by the promise of bargains. Other retailers of note in the picture include Noble's Card Company and the K Shoes shop.*
It is just possible to make out the premises of the Leeds Permanent Building Society on the right of the picture. The Riverhead Centre was later to be accessible via the small entrance on the right of the photograph, it's function would later be taken over by the new and impressive Freshney Place. Classic car buffs will recognise the Triumph 13/60 saloon car on the right of the picture. An improvement on the original Herald model it was the little sister of the sporty six-cylinder Vitesse.

A scene from part of the Old Market Place, looking in the direction of Grimsby Town Railway Station, in a photograph from the early 1960s. The large BASS sign denotes the location of the Pestle and Mortar public house with its very distinctive mock-tudor facade. A row of motorcars parked along the street reminds us of an era when parking restrictions were less oppressive than they are today. Interestingly, all the cars are British made, though the Ford Consul and Vauxhall models shown were clearly influenced by American styling. In the distance it is just possible to discern the corner of the Yarborough Hotel. Some idea of the time of year featured may be gleaned from the fairy lights strung across the lamposts from one end of the street to the other. These draw attention to the rather ugly, utilitarian street lamps themselves which were a common feature of many towns throughout Britain.

NELC Local History Collection

Above: To the casual observer this pleasant open area, with its thoughtfully positioned raised flower beds and parking spaces for about sixty vehicles, might have been planned this way. More mature Grimsby folk will be aware that this open space was created when the Corn Exchange was pulled down after around a century of loyal service to local shoppers. It had been built in 1854 along with a new Market Hall for the not inconsiderable sum of £3500. The Corn Exchange was constructed of red brick with decorative stone inserts and a fine hexagonal entrance.

Left: Fond memories are bound to be rekindled by this picture of Victoria Street West, taken when the usually busy parade of shops were eerily quiet. Most passers-by would be more interested in the products and services on offer along the street than the architecture of the buildings which housed them.

But spare a moment to study the different styles of the buildings on Victoria Street and the investment is soon rewarded. Plain modern facades designed to be functional and economical contrast sharply with the grand imposing architecture of the popular Building Society shown here. The ornate frontage was clearly designed to foster an image of reliability and stability. *Lawson and Stockdale's,* the highly respected department store is shown to the right of the building society offices. The property was later to house a retailer of even greater repute - Marks and Spencer. Woolworths could be found further along the street. Many local folk will remember acquiring their first pair of spectacles from Charnley's Opticians. The business was established at 45 Victoria Street West in 1906 by Mr G. W. Charnley. Later it was taken over by his two sons, Mssrs W.E. and J.E Charnley.

At leisure

Below right: One of Cleethorpes' proud boasts was that visitors to the resort would arrive there within yards of the sea front. This delightful 1930s picture shows hoards of excited holiday makers doing just that as they promenade past the Auckland Restaurant and absorb the atmosphere created by the exciting attractions. Among these attractions was *Pinchbecks Promenade,* their advertisement telling of 'foreign and live' animals and birds, along with a picture of a dancing bear. The moving targets on the rifle range provided fun for many a budding marksman, and *Wonderland* and the *Fairy River.* The silhouette of the area's industrial paraphernalia is clearly evident in this picture, making a stark contrast with the leisurely pace of life in the foreground.

Bottom: This busy scene is thought to date from the 1930s. It features thousands of visitors arriving at Cleethorpes - by rail of course - on a warm Bank Holiday.

The 1930s saw Cleethorpes achieve 'borough' status - an achievement which caused much rejoicing among local people as this was the first new borough to be created in Lincolnshire for 500 years! The charter marking the event was presented to Lord Heanage by Edward VIII in 1936.

At around the time this photograph was taken the Winter Gardens (originally known as 'Olympia') were opened. The facility provided indoor amusements including a rifle range and a sports stadium. After the war, in 1947 it was renovated and upgraded. The Marine Embankment was built in 1930 and 1933 saw the first illuminations in Cleethorpes, attracting visitors from long distances to see them.

NELC Local History Collection

A busy scene from the promenade at Cleethorpes which was captured for us back in the 1930s. This was considerably before the age of hot dogs and bingo, yet the resort was not short of ideas for fun and entertainment even in the 1930s. Bonny baby contests, beauty contests sports and donkey derbys were all on the agenda. Cleethorpes was one of the very first towns in the country to enjoy electric lighting. These were of the carbon arc type, set upon poles from the High Cliffe area to the bottom of Isaacs Hill in the year 1882. A couple of years later the railway was upgraded from a single line connecting the town with Grimsby to a multi-track line capable of carrying large numbers of passengers at peak times.

Left: Memories of summer holidays and day trips with our mams and dads come flooding back when we look at this picture. The exact date of origin of the photograph is unknown, but we can be virtually certain from the coach registration plate that it was taken before 1963 and the introduction of 'dated' number plates. The coach itself is wonderfully nostalgic with lavish amounts of bright chromework, curvaceous perspex windows and immaculate gleaming paintwork. The destination board suggests a Scottish tour though we cannot tell whether the journey had just ended or was about to begin. We can, however, be certain that this was Briggergate Bus Station - later to be taken over by Appleby's the well-known coach operators.

The origins of Granville tours can be traced back to 1913 and a small business established in Grimsby by Arthur and Alfred Blackbourne with the aid of a horse and cart. The modest business involved carting fish around Grimsby Docks. Hard work and shrewd dealing resulted in rapid growth. Within a year they were able to buy another three horse-drawn carts and soon motorised lorries were acquired. Passenger transport became an important part of the business from 1928 with the acquisition of a 14-seater charabanc. By 1945 there were 100 coaches in the firm's passenger fleet which operated nationally under the name *Granville Tours*.

Above: There could be few nicer places to imagine on a hot summers' day than the *Open Air Swimming Pool* at Cleethorpes. At times it was advertised as the largest such public facility in the world. Children would travel from miles around during the summer holidays and spend the day splashing around in the pool. Often the day would begin with a long walk to the pool - always preferable to spending the money on bus fares. Nobody seemed to mind the walk, provided that the weather stayed fine and the sun didn't burn too much. No sun cream in those days. Kids were always guaranteed to sleep soundly after the the days fun. One local lady remembers how summer passes could be bought in the 'big' school holiday, saying that she hardly saw her lively son for the whole six weeks, such was the attraction of the open air pool. The best days at the pool were those spent with all the family - usually with a picnic - when a combination of relaxation and excitement helped ease the burden of otherwise stressful lives.

Cleethorpes with holiday activity in full swing in the 1950s. This picture was probably taken on a Bank Holiday, when a combination of good weather and an excellent reputation could easily attract 10,000 visitors to the resort. This very nostalgic scene brings memories flooding back. The pier in the distance was a huge attraction despite being only 400 yds long and one of the shortest in the country. It was constructed in 1872 by a Stockton company at a cost of around £10,000. The pier opened on August Bank Holiday 1873 and attracted just short of 3000 visitors paying sixpence each. It was the arrival of the railway which began to establish Cleethorpes as a serious holiday resort. As well as providing the means for people to travel to the resort the railway companies also invested considerably in the town, including the purchase of a 17 acre site in 1882. Much investment was needed to equip Cleethorpes as a tourist centre, including improved sea defences costing £33,000 as far back as 1883.

A rooftop-view of the area around the Blundell Park home of Grimsby Town. A popular cinema can be seen at the bottom left of the photograph. The Mariners' first matches were played at Clee Park in the nineteenth century, but later a move to Abbey Park (near Wellholme Road and People's Park) took place. The moving didn't end there, for the owner of Abbey Park, Lord Heneage, turfed the club out of their 'new' home in 1898. Fortunately the Blundell Park site was spotted close to where the Imperial Hotel was to be built. The site was acquired and stands were removed from Abbey Park and re-erected in time for the first fixture. This took place on 2nd September 1898 and a 3 - 3 draw against Luton Town was the outcome. The proud history of the *Mariners* - Grimsby Town Association Football Club to give them their Sunday name - can be traced back to the 1870s. A meeting of local sports enthusiasts at the Wellington Arms on Freeman Street led to the creation of Grimsby Pelham Football Club, the name being taken from the Earl of Yarborough. Other teams competed for the right to represent the town in the official league but it was Grimsby Pelham F.C that would go on to become Grimsby Town Football Club in 1879.

This picture dates from around four decades ago and shows the Park ground bounded by Grimsby Road at the bottom of the picture and the railway sidings at the top. Railway paraphernalia in this area has been greatly reduced since the photograph was taken.

Football has been played at Blundell Park since September 1898, the ground taking its name from an adjacent residential avenue. This photograph gives a nostalgic view of the Hewitt Stand - now gone of course, and the tall floodlights which have illuminated league matches when necessary since 1960. One lifelong supporter reflected on some of the quieter moments at home games when a favourite pastime was counting the ships travelling up and down the river!

Wartime

Below: Sandbags were a central feature of Grimsby's air-raid precautions. Tons and tons and *tons,* of sand was packed into thousands of hessian sacks and piled up against civic buildings and public air raid shelters. This photograph was taken at the dawn of the Second World War on the public recreation ground near Doughty Road. It would have been back-breaking monotonous work for the volunteers pictured here as they toiled beneath the hot summer sun. At the beginning of the war there was understandable and widespread anxiety among the public as well as the government amid fears that the Nazis would attack the civilian population quickly. Gas masks and air raid shelters were issued and the mass evacuation of 1,300,000 children in vulnerable areas of the country took place immediately after war was declared. After many months the anticipated bombing had failed to materialise and the children were sent home.

Right: A photograph dating from around sixty years ago in the early years of the Second World War.

The location will quickly be recognised as Park Drive, the elaborate (and now removed) gateway in the background being a major clue. It was Autumn judging by the leaves on the kerbside, though there was still enough foliage to obscure the entrance to People's Park. Rooftops behind the wartime Bobby indicate the position of a large house. It would later become an old folks home which adopted the name Park Gates. Clearly the main subject for this picture was the large ambulance. Saloon cars or light commercial vehicles were often converted for war use into transportation which performed a wide variety of functions.

Conversions from saloon cars to vans, ambulances, water carriers and fire tenders were relatively common in the war years.

The task was easier than it would be today, thanks to the saloon cars having a strong separate frame (chassis) on which the body was mounted. The white-walled tyres of this ambulance would have complemented the other white markings which were designed to aid road safety during the blackout.

NEL Museums

Wartime Grimsby is featured in this rare picture. The clues as to the photograph's wartime origins are numerous: Headlamps are painted out because of the strict blackout regulations; the light van on the left of the scene is marked ARP (standing for air-raid precautions of course) and a group of soldiers can be seen walking away from the camera, virtually in the centre of the photograph, to the right of Turners large drapers store. A lovely view of the old Corn Exchange and the old market buildings is afforded by the picture and a large thermometer-style fund-raising sign is attached to it. The sign relates to one of the many campaigns designed to raise money for the war effort. This campaign was called 'Salute the Soldier' and was run throughout Britain simul-taneously. The White Hart public house stands in the foreground on the right of the picture as the stalls on the open market conduct a brisk trade in the Old Market Place.

Above: The substantial and delightfully-styled houses along Park Drive provide a timeless backdrop for this 1940s photograph. It records some of the assets of the wartime civil defence authorities which had been proudly assembled and photographed. The vehicles in question were converted from their original use so as to perform specific wartime functions. At the head of the 'convoy' was a converted single-decker bus, its new function as an A.R.P ambulance being obvious from the converted destination board at the front. Rationing was a wartime phenomenon that would have been familiar to the people in this picture. It had been introduced in January 1940 initially applying to butter, sugar and bacon but eventually most staple foods were included. Parks and flower beds were ploughed up and vegetables planted there. At least 80,000 women joined the Womens Land Army, many of them in the agricultural areas around Grimsby, and Britain adopted the slogan "Dig for Victory."

Right: These delightful ladies were part of the workforce tasked with keeping Grimsby's bus service operational during the war years. From May 1940 control over manpower (and *woman* power!) rested in the hands of Ernest Bevin M.P - the Minister of Labour.

It was estimated that a million and a half women would be needed to support wartime production of arms and munitions as well as food production and the maintenance of public services such as 'the buses.' From March 1941 the compulsory registration of women commenced and eventually all women between the ages of 18 and 60 were expected to work as part of the war effort. For most, if not all women, the work was welcomed. Good money good be earned and the war virtually eliminated unemployment.

Women were given responsibility, a sense of purpose and camaraderie which some had never experienced before.

A very nostalgic atmosphere is created by this picture which shows Maddisons Corner located at the junction of Pasture Street and Victoria Street. According to the notice on the elaborately-painted wall, Maddisons were the cake shop 'with a reputation.' Just over the way (Pasture Street) from Maddisons there was a town centre police telephone box which was used by Bobbies on the town centre beat. They could also be used by members of the public to report incidents or fires to the authorities. Along Victoria Street the Baptist Tabernacle can be seen. This is a wartime photograph, and much of the 'street furniture' such as street lamps and road signs etc. has had white stripes painted around it in order to aid visibility in the blackout.

NEL Museums

Left: Utter devastation was caused by enemy bombs falling on Grimsby on a number of occasions. This morning-after scene dates from 1942 and features the remains of South Parade School and the damaged housing stock in the surrounding area. It was a terrifying time for residents in any town which was the target of regular enemy raids. By the end of the six-year conflict more than 6000 local houses and commercial properties had either been destroyed or damaged. More than 700 air-raid warnings - signified by the distinctive wartime sirens - had been made, and almost 180 Grimsby folk (including 28 Public Service personnel) had lost their lives in the raids.

Above: When these houses were destroyed by a Nazi bomb in 1942 the optimism and resolve of the residents of Hope Street was tested to the extreme. Grimsby endured several enemy bomb attacks between August 1940 and July 1943. There is no doubt that many lives were saved as a result of the distribution of public and domestic air-raid shelters and use of anti-blast tape criss crossed over glass windows throughout the town. There were fears - probably stemming from memories of injuries caused by Mustard Gas in the First World War - that the Germans would use poisoned gas on the civilian population. Gas masks were issued to every man, woman and child - even babies were provided with the devices. It became a legal requirement for citizens to carry the masks with them at all times. In the event there never was a gas attack on British soil during the conflict.

This atmospheric scene reminds us of how Grimsby town centre appeared in the dark days of the Second World War. This was the top of Victoria Street of course, and shoppers and workers can be seen dodging the traffic as they make their way home after a busy day. The number 3 bus approaching the camera has blacked-out lights and white-painted strips as a road safety aid. There were thousands of civilian injuries during the war caused by the people bumping into things or falling over in the dark conditions. People would 'wear something white' or leave their shirt tail hanging out as recommended by Government advice - but the accidents continued. A good view of the lost and much-lamented Corn Exchange is afforded. On the left of the picture a fascia sign above the shop property has the words 'Not Rationed' written along it. Next door to that establishment was Atkinsons the menswear shop. Trade would have been difficult for any menswear shop with the restrictions on clothing sales and the fact that so many men were away fighting the war.

L.O.R - Power at the heart of the region

Lindsey Oil Refinery is the third largest refinery in Britain in terms of crude oil refining capacity, with a throughput approaching ten million tonnes per annum. It owes its continuing success to a combination of high calibre personnel (some of the best in the industry), sophisticated technology, and an unrivalled location on the Humber estuary.

Back in 1963, Total Oil (Great Britain) Ltd - the UK division of France's biggest oil and gas group, whose interests stretch across the globe - realised that its wide-ranging distribution and marketing business in this country would be ideally served by a dedicated UK refinery. The logic was unassailable, but where to site it? Many factors play a part in these decisions. It was important that the new refinery should be near to healthy markets, in an area amply served by transport communications - both for the inward arrival of crude and for the outward journey of refined products -, that a good local labour force would be available for recruitment and specialist training and, perhaps most pressing of all, that suitable

and affordable land could be found for the development. With these concerns in mind, the advantages of the Humber estuary soon became clear. Its location on the North Sea provided ready access to and from Northern Europe, and

Above: The new refinery quickly became a major landmark, particularly at night.
Below: Process Unit looking North West in February 1967.

Rotterdam in particular, while its proximity to much of the North and Midlands of England offered an unrivalled potential to exploit the market demand from the Trent power stations and neighbouring Gas Board reforming plants. There was deep-water access, suitable for ocean-going tankers, in a region - unlike, say, Milford Haven - where no refinery yet existed. The scope for developing new markets in the swelling industrial conurbations of the East Midlands and Yorkshire was also attractive, given the rapid improvements in road, rail and water links that were then underway in Humberside. And best of all - extensive areas of land were available for industrial development. In June 1964, Total announced that Immingham would soon witness the birth of a massive new Company.

Other oil companies, meanwhile, were having similar ideas and, like Total, had already identified the benefits of the Immingham area. Discussions began with the Belgian group, Petrofina, and by February 1965, a partnership deal was struck: a refinery twice the size of the one originally envisaged would now be constructed, with Total holding 50% of the shareholding and Petrofina (later Fina plc) taking the other 50%.

No time was lost in taking up options on 1800 acres of land and soon the site's development programme was underway. A mind-boggling two million tons of earth had to be moved as a first task, but by January 1966 construction could begin at North Killingholme. Since then four separate stages of construction and expansion have followed.

A dynamic core team of managers, engineers and supervisors was assembled from refineries all over the world. Their goal was to not only to build and commission a state-of-the-art refinery complex, but also to recruit and train a work force from the local region who would be equipped to operate it and, in the years to come, to meet the expert tasks of management and supervisory roles themselves. It is a testament not only to the original crack team but also to the dedication and skill of the local personnel that Lindsey Oil Refinery, or LOR as it is better known, has proved to be the success story it is today, a key player in the region's economy and firmly at the heart of the local community.

But what exactly does an oil refinery do? What emerges from an oil well is crude oil. It is seldom used without refining, although in countries where natural seepages occur people have for centuries applied it for medicinal purposes, both externally and (perhaps alarming to us!) internally. In desert regions it has also long been regarded as an effective treatment for mange in camels. Crude oil, like all natural resources, comes

Above: Lindsey Oil Refinery Ltd in Killingholme which dates to 1967.

in a variety of forms, but each one is made up of a range of hydrocarbons, offering distinct chemical properties, together with a mixture of other compounds. The refining process distills the raw product into a series of 'fractions', the light, medium and heavy hydrocarbons which provide the most useful constituents of crude oil - and subject them to further treatment in order to derive specific products. Lighter hydrocarbons, for example, generate bottle-gas and Naphtha (which after further processing becomes petrol), the heavier fraction comprises kerosene, jet fuel, diesel and central heating oil, whilst the heavier fraction is destined for the production of Bitumen and the fuel needs of industry.

In May 1968, the refinery was on-stream with a relatively simple 'hydro-skimmer' system producing a complete range of petroleum products - exclusively for Total - at the rate of 3.3 million tonnes per year. Stage Two followed soon afterwards and was operational by January 1970; this provided Petrofina with a duplicate Crude Distillation Unit together with additional facilities enabling LOR to tackle a wider range of crudes.

The decade that followed witnessed turbulent changes in the oil industry. In 1973, the Arab-Israeli War resulted in a sudden cut-off in oil supplies from the Middle East - a time many of us remember clearly, coinciding as it did with disputes in the coal industry and ushering in a long winter of enforced energy conservation - reduced speed limits on our roads, the three-day week, chillier work-places and town centre streets plunged at night into unfamiliar, unlit darkness. The crisis over, political and market forces saw a rapid rise in the price of crude oil. Demand for fuel oil suffered a decline, whilst the demand for petrol and diesel increased steadily. The way ahead for LOR became clear: further major expansion was needed to enable the refinery to convert much of the fuel oil and LPG produced by the crude units directly into petrol products, for which there was now so much demand. Work started at the end of 1977 on what was to be the third, and most sophisticated, stage of the Refinery's expansion, with the construction of a

Above: One of Lindsey Oil Refinery's process columns arriving at Immingham Dock after fabrication in Europe.

demand for liquid sulphur for the chemical industry. This complex period of development ended in the first half of 1981 when the new technology became operational.

Stage Four came hot on its heels. This saw the addition of a Visbreaker Unit (able to extract Naphtha and gas oil from the heavy fractions produced by the vacuum distillation units) and a Catalytic Polymerisation Unit which provided the Refinery with the

Fluid Catalytic Cracking Unit and Vacuum Distillation Unit, also a second larger sulphur recovery unit that simultaneously cut sulphur dioxide emissions and supplied the increasing

Above: The fluid catalytic cracking unit under construction.
Below: An aerial view of the refinery today.

electricity needs, providing an alternative power supply and ensuring the maximum reliability of operation.

The higher efficiency of this unit compared to traditional means of producing electricity and steam increases LOR's overall energy efficiency, giving both a reduction in operating costs and a reduction in emissions to atmosphere.

capacity for generating a high octane blending component used in petrol. This new development was in service by mid-1983.

Always quick to identify trends in the market, and leading the way in harnessing new technology, LOR has never sat on its laurels. A combination of ideal location and typically enterprising management saw it at the forefront of developments after the UK uncovered its most precious natural resources in two hundred years - under the North Sea. LOR was the first refinery to process North Sea Oil and to this day derives a large part of its feedstock (or crude oil) from that source. Similar foresight guaranteed an early move into the market for unleaded petrol. A £20 million investment programme saw the opening, in March 1987, of two new plants which enable high octane unleaded motor spirit to be produced, not only eliminating lead emissions, as the new 'green' motorist demands, but also significantly reducing carbon monoxide emissions.

In 1995, LOR entered into partnership with National Power to construct a £21 million Combined Heat and Power Plant.

Using clean technology with natural gas as fuel, the plant provides much needed flexibility to steam supplies and meets all the refinery's

Full commercial operation started as planned in December 1996, producing 40 mW of electricity, of which 26 mW is exported to the National Grid, and up to 140 tonnes of steam per hour used by the refinery.

The transport requirements to supply LOR with its 10 million tonnes of feedstock and to distribute its refined products are astonishing, incorporating rail, road, pipelines and marine. The proximity of the Humber was an advantage, but the estuary had not previously dealt with large tankers and an early challenge for the new enterprise in 1964, even before the first shovelful of earth was shifted on the Killingholme site, was to build deep-water berthing facilities, suitable for crude oil carriers, just off the shore near Immingham. To this end, in late 1964, Total, Fina and Conoco (another oil company investing in the Humber area) formed a joint company, to be known as Associated Petroleum Terminals (APT), to operate the jetty. The first section of the new jetty was

"LOR WAS THE FIRST REFINERY TO PROCESS NORTH SEA OIL"

Above: Mr Graham Brown, Commercial Director of National Power, pictured with LOR's General Manager Quentin de Borrekens, at the official opening of the CHP Plant in spring 1997.

commissioned in April 1969, importing 31,000 tonnes of Algerian crude to LOR. So as to take full advantage of the deep water channel, the jetty stretches for approximately 1,000 yards into the river. Each of the two main berths is able to accommodate two 100,000 tonne tankers, or a part-laden Very Large Crude Carrier (part-laden because of the draft restrictions on the river). One of the largest vessels to berth there was a 290,000 tonne dead weight vessel, carrying 140,000 tonnes of crude oil from Iran. When a tanker of crude oil arrives, the cargo is unloaded directly into a crude pipeline situated alongside, measuring 36" in diameter. The oil is then pumped to LOR, some 4.5 miles away, at a rate of up to 10,000,000 litres per hour! Refinery and jetty are also connected by further pipelines designed for motor spirit, kerosene and gas oil, and also by insulated fuel lines. By these means, not only is crude readily transferred for processing, but finished products can straightfor-wardly be piped back - for delivery by ship. By 1981, the Immingham Oil Terminal was reaching capacity just as Stage Three of the Refinery's

expansion was coming on line, and it was at this time that the South Killingholme Jetty, came into its own handling liquid petroleum gas (LPG) and white oils. In 1985, two LPG storage caverns, situated 200 metres below ground, came into operation - and the Immingham Gas Jetty, designed at first to handle LPG, but later modified to take white oils as well, was also established.

Above: More help for special needs with a cheque from LOR. Below: Many local charities have benefited from the Safety Charity Scheme.

The terminal has become one of the busiest in the UK, handling almost 50% of the 45 million tonnes moved through Immingham Docks.

The remaining 75% of refined products are distributed by road (20%), rail (28%) and pipeline (27%). The road loading facility, Killingholme Road Loading, is managed by Total on behalf of both Shareholders. They operate 38 loading bays accommodating over 400 road tankers each day delivering to a wide range of companies. The rail loading complex constitutes the largest private rail complex in the UK, with 13 miles of sidings and rail track. The rail loading facility loads up to five trains simultaneously, filling a 100 tonne rail car in a mere 15 minutes at the rate of 6,000 litres per minute! In 1991 distribution from the Refinery was dramatically improved with the opening of a 225km (nearly 150 miles) line to Fina's Buncefield Terminal in Hertfordshire. The Fina-Line transports to the large markets of the London conurbation and the South East.

These impressive statistics demonstrate a vigorous enthusiasm at LOR for technological and systems excellence - but, however sophisticated a plant might be in terms of its capital investment, it is only the people who work together at its heart that can guarantee the overall success of the

Below: The combined heat and power plant utilising clean technology to produce steam and electricity.

Refinery. LOR has, from the very beginning, put people first - a sense of teamwork was fostered in the early days which has strengthened and matured into a culture of genuine cooperation throughout the Refinery's personnel. The staff level for LOR and APT is surprisingly small - barely 550 - and demands considerable adaptability from the workforce. A strong emphasis on development and training ensures that every individual is skilled in all essential tasks at the Refinery - and this in itself provides a ready impetus for promotion. While more technical roles tend to be filled from outside the region, LOR has made a virtue of taking on local people, many with no previous refining experience or professional qualification, and developing their talents so effectively that an entire career can be nurtured on site. In fact, many locally recruited staff have, over the years, been able to rise through the ranks to positions of seniority - an old-fashioned value that other companies might usefully take up! It's an environment where people thrive - staff turnover is reassuringly low; there are even examples of people temporarily leaving the region only to leap straight back if a suitable vacancy occurs at LOR!

The foundation of well-trained and committed employees supports the three management systems, for Safety, Environment and Quality. An excellent performance in these is an essential prerequisite for the success of any company. At LOR and APT, these systems meet the highest international standards.

ISRS, the International Safety Rating System, ranks LOR's Safety Management System amongst top 5% of UK Industry, and the Company is proud of its reputation for safe operation which has been established with both staff and neighbours over many years.

In 1993, LOR's Environmental Management System was brought in line with the International Standard now known as ISO 14001, and was given full certification in 1995. It was the first company on Humberside to achieve this recognition, and the first Refinery in the UK to meet this rigorous standard.

The protection of the environment receives the very highest priority throughout the activities of LOR's workforce, and this goal is enshrined in the form of a Policy statement. An ongoing investment programme of sophisticated monitoring and control systems, water treatment

and gas cleaning systems ensures that words are always backed up by deeds. In the past decade alone, LOR has invested over £42 million in projects benefiting the environment, and future projects totalling a further £18 million have already been identified. The concerns of local people are recognised and met through the formation of the Killingholme Environmental Liaison Committee, which provides a vital link between the local community and the Refinery.

The Quality Management System ensures that LOR's Shareholders receive high quality products to supply to their customers. It was approved under ISO 9002 in 1991, making LOR one of the first refineries in the UK to receive this recognition.

Over the past 35 years, LOR has become established as a major contributor to the local economy. Its influence as an employer, either directly or indirectly via the thousands of contractors and suppliers who rely on the Refinery for their livelihood, is enormous.

LOR is confident that with the support and commitment of its staff, they will continue their role as a dynamic powerhouse for the whole region, and beyond.

Above: Looking through the large pipes a scene of the refinery.

Events & occasions

Below: The war was over and the citizens of Grimsby were tired of bombs, gas masks and the blackout. The entire community went wild with joy when the news that everyone was waiting for was announced. Bunting was strung from house to house across the streets, patriotic flags floated gently in the breeze and 'Welcome Home' notices were painted to greet the returning troops. It was good to be alive and, along with the rest of Britain they found the energy to let their hair down and organise a knees-up after six long years of war. This scene was repeated throughout Britain, but it was the new Prime Minister, Clement Attlee, who brought the nation down to earth with a bump. He warned the country that although Britain was once more at peace, there was no likelihood of prosperity for the country in the immediate future. There would be worldwide food shortages and it would be several more years before people could stop relying on tinned dried eggs or shop for clothes without using their coupons.

NELC Local History Collection

Above: Dancing in the street was an uncommon sight in Grimsby and it is likely that a particularly persuasive photographer was responsible for staging this scene. It is known that the location of the shot was Cosgrove Street but the event being celebrated is less certain. A clue to this may be found in the fancy dress being worn by some of the participants.
In the foreground a little lad can be seen dancing with his chum, dressed in what looks like a King's Coronation robes. Could this have been a coronation party? If so the date is likely to have been 1936 when George V succeeded his brother, Edward VII who had decided to abdicate because of his love of American divorcee Mrs Simpson. There was relief in the country when the constitutional crisis passed and the coronation of the former Duke of York (and father of our present queen) took place.

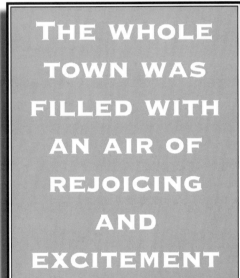

NEL Museums

THE WHOLE TOWN WAS FILLED WITH AN AIR OF REJOICING AND EXCITEMENT

children - many of whom had no memory of the days before shortages or rationing. The whole town filled with an air of rejoicing and excitement; fireworks, saved from before the war, were set off; buildings were illuminated and giant 'V' for victory signs appeared every-where. Of course, the celebrations were tinged with sadness and thoughts of the brave men and women, both at home and abroad, who had lost their lives during the conflict.

Left: News of the unconditional surrender of the Nazi war machine was the cause of unprecedented celebrations throughout Britain. Grimsby, which had felt more than its fair share of the effects of the war, gladly threw itself into party mood with the rest of the country. It was May 1945 and this picture taken on First Avenue on the Nunsthorpe Estate shows one of the hundreds of street parties held for the children of the area. Everyone 'pulled together' to put on a fine spread for the local

Above: Practically every child residing along Hope Street was summoned for a celebratory photograph in 1945 as the whole country rejoiced at the end of the war. Of course, most of them had known nothing but wartime conditions during their short lifetimes, with all the worry, rationing and fear of enemy bombing raids that went with it. Hope Street was a casualty of one of those bombing raids but the Nazis were unable to suppress the wartime spirit that epitomised the *Grimbarians* who lived there.

Above: *Crowd control* was the order of the day when Prince Philip visited Grimsby in 1949. The crowd in question was good-humoured and had assembled in Town Hall Square and when the royal visitor was inside the Town Hall enjoying lunch with the mayor and civic officials.

He had arrived at *Grimsby Town* station at 8.00 am and spent the morning visiting groups and organisations involved in the fishing industry. Local newspaper reports from the time told of the prince's 'ready chat and easy manner' which set the whole of Grimsby cheering. Prince Philip went aboard the *Rinovia* the most modern Grimsby fishing vessel at the time which had just returned from a 24 day fishing trip. At the end of his visit the prince was escorted by police to Binbrook Aerodrome from where he flew back to London.

Inset: A very special visitor listened attentively as the workings of this Grimsby Smoke House were explained to him. The picture dates from 1948 and the V.I.P was a youthful HRH Duke of Edinburgh. The timing of the visit is significant,

NELC Local History Collection

GRIMSBY DRY FISH CHARGED 5/- RETURN TO GRIMSBY

being just three years after the end of the war and at the dawn of the very rapid expansion of fish processing factories in Grimsby. The processing of fish began in the 1920s when the filleting of fish prior to distribution became the norm.

The practice made a lot of sense, with benefits such as the elimination of the need to transport the inedible parts of the fish as well as the opportunity to convert this otherwise wasted offal into useful white fish meal.

Food production was at the forefront of national concerns in 1948. Shortages and rationing still prevailed at this time and did so well into the 1950s. The national economy was struggling to get back on its feet after running up huge wartime debts.

The task of satisfying domestic demand for food products was addressed by the food processing firms in and around Grimsby. Exports were another pre-occupation of the nation, and the Port of Grimsby was destined to play a vital role in that respect. These factors combined to boost the importance of Grimsby to the regional and national economy.

Above: In July 1949 Grimsby had the honour of an official visit by HRH Prince Philip. At the time there was little for most people to smile about; the country was struggling to get back on her feet after the end of the war, taxes were at a high level and many products and foodstuffs were still in short supply. Shortly before the visit clothing came off coupon restrictions. Nearer home a programme of house building had been set in motion and around 1300 houses had been built in the four-year period. The Prince is pictured with Grimsby's first Lady Mayoress, Alderman Margaret Larmour and the well-known local figure Sir Reginald Hill as the party walk toward the Fish Pontoon.

Right: The flags were out and people squeezed on the platform of the railway footbridge to gain a better view when Prince Philip visited Grimsby in 1949. Close scrutiny reveals the Prince standing with Grimsby's first lady mayor in the centre of the picture. In the distance the grey outline of the old Dock Offices can be seen and a row of shiny limousines on the right of the picture is parked outside the Fish Workers Canteen. Still in the centre of the photograph, but slightly nearer to the camera, a newsreel photographer and a colleague can be seen preparing their equipment. Police officers are in evidence but the level of security is less than we would expect in modern times for a royal visitor to a public place.

THOUSANDS OF LOYAL SUBJECTS JOURNEYED BY TRAIN TO SEE THE CORONATION OF QUEEN ELIZABETH II

The coronation of HM Queen Elizabeth II was a reason for tremendous national celebration throughout the land. The decorations in London were elaborate and widely reported in the national press. Understandably there was intense interest in the occasion and thousands of loyal subjects journeyed by rail to either see the decorations or witness the coronation itself. Few people were as lucky as those pictured here, all workers from *Dixons Paper Mills*, who travelled to London by train at the company's expense. These are just a few of the 800 people who made the trip, all well wrapped up against the weather and looking forward to the day ahead.

NEL Museums

Left: We can only guess at why the gentleman in this photograph thought his short-trousered suit was an appropriate way of celebrating the coronation of Queen Elizabeth. Still, his knobbly-knees earned him the attention of a passing photographer and, ultimately, a place in this book. The location of the picture was Hope Street with its distinctive brick-work and reputation for the best home made decorations in Grimsby. Hope Street was pulled down in 1971 and many residents were re-housed in modern tower blocks around the town. These were equipped with modern heating, kitchens and bathrooms etc., but lacked the ability to foster the sense of community which had been enjoyed by Hope Street residents for generations.

Above: The residents of Hope Street had a well-earned and now well-known reputation for 'pushing the boat out' at times of national celebrations. As a consequence the area was always first on the list for local press photographers and agencies wishing to record scenes on a 'typical' Grimsby street whenever there was serious celebrating to be done. Of course, the extent of Hope Street's decorations and merry-making were far from typical. Each new occasion became a challenge to the residents on the humble but proud row of terraced houses; reputations had to be maintained and increasingly elaborate ways of decorating the street found. The celebrations featured here relate to the coronation of Queen Elizabeth II. The popularity of the queen, her handsome husband and young family was enormous. The coronation is memorable for another reason, for it was the State occasion to be covered extensively by the new medium of television. Sets were few and far between in Grimsby, but those lucky enough to to own one soon found a houseful of friends and relatives willing to watch the event with them.

NEL Museums

Above: A very proud day for the people of Grimsby was recorded in this photograph from June 1958. Her Majesty the Queen, HRH Duke of Edinburgh and Grimsby's popular Mayor Alderman Matt Larmour walk on the obligatory red carpet as thousands of cheering Grimbarians look on. A busy schedule was in store for the royal party which included an inspection of a modern Grimsby fishing vessel, the *MT Rhodesian* and the opening of the King George V playing fields. In addition, representatives from all sections of the fishing industry were presented to the visitors, along with workers at the various organisations concerned. The royal party had arrived in Grimsby at 10.00 am, aboard the Royal Barge which was moored at the docks. Her Majesty was asked to approve a gift of fish was sent to the ship's company aboard Britannia. The visit lasted until 12.30 pm, and the convoy of gleaming limousines travelled via Weelsby Road, Bargate, Old Market, Victoria Street and Town Hall Street much to the delight of their cheering subjects.

Down at the docks

Below: The interest in fish and fishing which has characterised the menfolk of Grimsby for centuries is clearly evident in this picture! Fishing at River Head was a favourite pastime and a gentle introduction to the industry which would dominate the lives of some of the lads shown here. The photograph dates from 1937, meaning that at the time of writing all the youngsters will be well past retirement age, having lived through a world war, seen the birth of the television age and the first steps taken by man on the Moon. It is virtually certain that some relatives of these boys would have been involved in Grimsby's fishing industry. Perhaps some were away at distant fishing grounds such as the Faroes, Iceland or the White Sea - enduring 3000 mile round-trips in all conditions to put fish in Britain's larders.

THE THIRD OF GRIMSBY'S DOCKS WAS OPENED IN 1934 AT A COST OF £1,650,000

wives gathered to open a new section of the facility. The third of Grimsby's fish docks was opened in 1934 at a cost of £1,650,000. It meant that a much-needed additional area of water amounting to 35 acres was made available which virtually doubled its capacity.

Below: Life aboard 'modern' fishing vessels had progressed significantly by the 1960s. One of the more pronounced developments came in the form of effective wireless sets which were a step forward in terms of safety. This picture shows equipment in the wireless room of a Grimsby fishing vessel.

Left: This was the scene at the end of the *old* Pontoon when some local company directors and their

Left: A birds-eye view of the docks area and the expanse of tightly-packed terraced houses in the distance. This are endured severe bomb damage during the Nazi raids of the Second World War. Grimsby's first proper dock was built between 1855 and 1857. The project cost £12,000 and was financed by the Midland Scottish and London Railway company. The second dock, covering 11 acres opened in 1877 after the same railway company invested a further £23,000 in the scheme. At this time around 50,000 tons of fish per year were landed in Grimsby and the railway was the obvious method of distribution for this valuable cargo. By 1934 Dock 3 was opened in order to cope with the increasing volumes of trade through Grimsby's port.

Below: A 1960s view of the back of the Pontoon in the Fish Market. The insulated containers look crude by modern standards, 'strapped' as they were to the back of these flimsy single-axle trailers. They would be loaded, then collected by tractor units for distribution throughout the country. Prior to 1964 the majority of the fish landed at Grimsby was distributed to Britain's markets by rail. The appointment of Dr. Beeching and his mission to 'make the railways pay' sounded alarm bells among Grimsby fish merchants. Beeching decided to phase out the fish train services upon which the industry relied. Under the scheme Grimsby fish was carried on an average of 300 railway vans per day on 9 special trains which served 4000 U.K railway stations.

The potential crisis was averted by the foundation of The Grimsby Fish Merchants Association and their work with the road haulier *British Road Services* which created a road-based distribution network for Grimsby fish. One advantage of the new system was that customers throughout Britain benefited from a door-to-door distribution service for the first time ever. The undertaking was a considerable one, with a total of 150,000 miles travelled each week by the substantial team of drivers.

NEL Museums

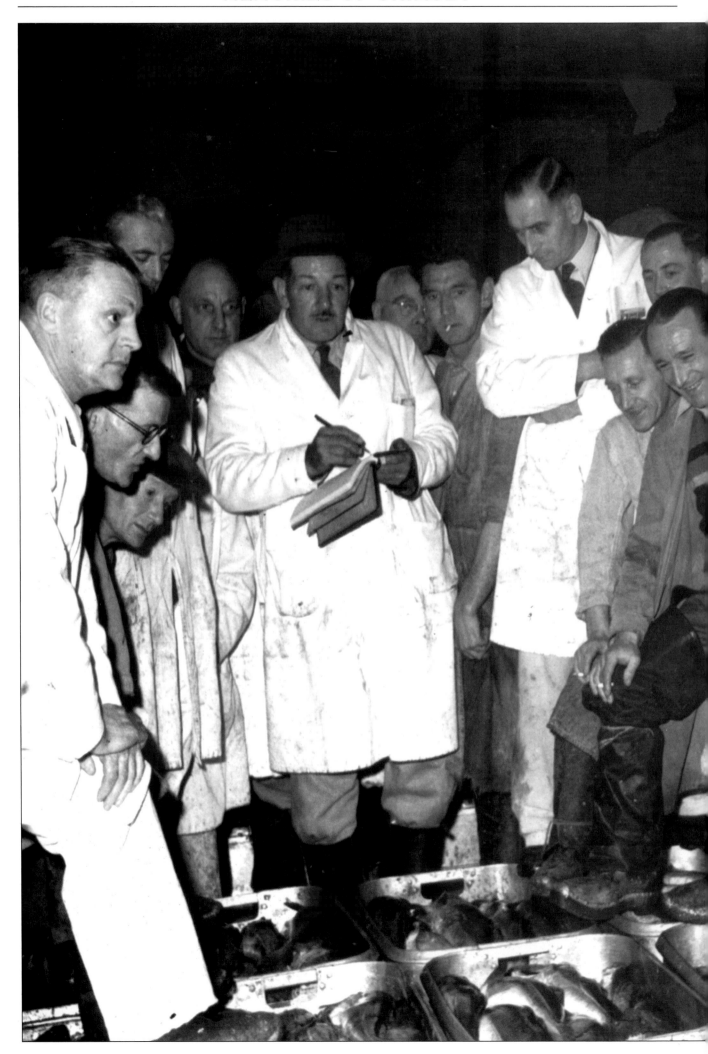

An early-morning sale at the old fish market was captured for posterity in this photograph from the late 1950s. At that time there were approximately 500 Grimsby fish merchants, ranging from the very small operators battling to make a living, to large national and international concerns. Typically, landings would be made at midnight and the fish would be set out in large aluminium containers as shown here. Merchants would inspect the fish before the sale began at 7.30 a.m. The first fish to be sold would be catches landed from distant waters and the auctioneer would progress through to catches from closer fishing grounds. Visitors to the fish market have always been impressed by the speed at which the sales take place and the way that communication between buyer and sellers appears to rely on telepathy. The speed is necessary because of the need to keep the fish fresh as it travels from supplier to consumer. This picture was taken in the old fish market before it was swept away and replaced by the modern but less characterful facility.

NEL Museums

Left: Grimsby's fishing fleet has always relied upon an army of skilled support workers carrying on a multitude of traditional trades on-shore. Net making is one of the most obvious of these and the photograph features a pretty young lady working as a Net Braider in one of the factories on Ropery Street. It is thought that the picture was taken just a decade or so after the end of the Second World War. Women have always been a vital element of the local economy in Grimsby. A journal from the 1950s described the fact rather patronisingly to modern eyes: "Grimsby's women and girl labour has been found excellently fitted for the manufacture of clothing and foodstuffs - industries which demand intelligence, nimbleness of finger and cleanliness of habit." These comments were designed to attract prospective employers into Grimsby to join the growing number of industrialists trading there.

Below: This striking night-time view of the Dock Tower is certain to stir feelings of pride and nostalgia in any native of Grimsby. A combination of factors resulted in the growth of the town's importance as a fishing port, but perhaps the most influential was the interest shown in the area by the railways. Commercial success was assured when the town became linked by rail with ready markets throughout Britain. Almost a century before they were nationalised, the privately-owned railway companies attracted huge amounts of capital and directed investment towards building some of Grimsby's docks. The Royal Dock was opened in 1852 by Queen Victoria and was capable of handling vessels of up to 400 ft in length. The Alexandra Dock opened in 1879 and came to specialise in handling timber. The second half of the eighteenth century saw massive growth in the local fishing industry with an accompanying growth in the local population. Another important milestone was the introduction of the steam trawler which, by 1914, had all but taken over from the traditional fishing smack. By 1939 Grimsby's docks and quays covered an area of 500 acres and had associated covered warehousing amounting to 525,000 square feet.

NELC Local History Collection

Right: Speed is of the essence when it comes to processing fresh fish for quick freezing. This is as true today as it was almost half a century ago when this picture was taken at a leading Grimsby frozen food processing company. This group of ladies took a breather from their normally lively conversation as the photographer recorded them at work, sometime during the 1950s. Their job involved weighing the filleted fish before it was rapidly packed and sent to the quick-freezing area. Hygiene was as important as speed, hence the spotless overalls and carefully covered hair. Fortunes were built upon the efforts of the skilled Grimsby workers in the relatively new frozen food industry which dispatched fish fingers, frozen peas and other popular foodstuffs throughout Britain.

Below: The Royal National Mission to Deep Sea Fishermen was a worthy institution, ready, willing and able to get unlucky fishermen back on their sea legs. The Queen Mary Hostel stood firm and proud along Orwell Street, its impressive exterior symbolising a degree of stability and security which the troubled seamen it cared for could only dream of. In recent times there has been talk of pulling down the well-known landmark This would be a sad end indeed for an institution which has done so much good. Character is added to the photograph by the presence of four or five motor cars from the late 1950s. Two of the vehicles, a Hillman Minx and a Hillman Husky (the small estate-type car near the corner) were products of the Rootes Group. A shiny black Rover P4 was easily the pick of the crop here; well-equipped and beautifully trimmed in walnut and leather it would have been the transport of company directors and bank managers throughout the land.

The Grimsby Docks Centenary Exhibition was held in September 1956. The event represented the largest fishing exhibition ever seen in Britain and its success was attributed to the co-operation of all sections of the industry. Major manufacturing operations were thrown open to the public. Warships from countries as diverse as Belgium, Poland, Sweden and Holland visited the port and allowed visitors to clamber over the vessels as part of the exhibition. Two Royal Navy ships attended as did an R.N.L.I lifeboat along with two state-of-the-art modern Grimsby trawlers. Visitors to the Centenary Exhibition may also remember seeing Donald Campbell's Blue Bird, indeed, Donald Campbell had the honour of opening the event much to the delight of every local schoolboy.

On the move

THE RAILWAY FOOTBRIDGE AT WELLOWGATE PROVIDED RELIEF FROM THE DELAYS CAUSED BY THE LEVEL CROSSING

occasion was the visit of HRH Prince Philip.

Below: A delightful picture from the 1950s reminds us of an era, almost half a century ago, when the railway footbridge at Wellowgate provided some relief (for pedestrians at least) from the long delays caused by the level crossing on this busy stretch of road. Passers-by in the picture appear to be well wrapped up against the weather with fashionable A-line coats and furry ankle boots much in evidence. The grey outline of the *Yarborough Hotel* can be seen in the distance. To the right, obscured by the structures in the foreground, stood the busy bus station operated by *Granville Tours*.

Left: Mugs of hot tea were the order of the day in the *Fish Workers Canteen* in 1949. The workers shown here were dressed in their smart suits and coats as a mark of respect for a royal visitor, for the

NEL Museums

NEL Museums

Left: Passengers await their connection at Grimsby Town Station, sometime in the 1960s. At first glance the station seems little changed, with the distinctive glass and iron roof covering the draughty platform below. Countless holiday excursions began and ended at Grimsby Town and nostalgic memories of the age of steam are never too far away when we visit the station. The Railway Age came to Grimsby with the arrival of the *Great Grimsby and Sheffield Railway Company* and the first rail link in 1848. The railway allowed Grimsby to break free from the restrictions of an isolated port and trade began to flourish. Wealthy railway companies began to invest in the docks, shrewdly foreseeing the enormous potential that the port's unique characteristics held for them.

Above: A massive rail-mounted crane is shown at work in 1932, with a small group of workmen and officials looking on from a sensible distance. The crane was of impressive proportions - it had to be in order to cope with the task of setting the occasional engine back on the tracks or lifting heavy railway equipment. A routine task would involve manoeuvring large sections of new bridges into place. This was the situation featured here when the Humber Street Bridge was under construction. Soon the bridge would begin easing the flow of traffic to the newly-created Fish Dock.

NELC Local History Collection

NELC Local History Collection

export markets. Britain had run up large debts during the war and exports were the natural way to pay for them. Grimsby was to benefit from the policy as the docks were a useful gateway for goods en-route to world markets.

Left: The traditional gift of a Christmas tree can be seen arriving at Grimsby Docks in the 1960s. The Butter Boat traders donated the tree each year to the people of Grimsby as a symbol of the strong links between the two communities.

Facing page: Loading a heavy saloon car on to a vessel in the Commercial Dock took considerable skill and care if the vehicle body was to pass though undamaged. Note the crude but effective large sacks used for this purpose which protected each mudguard from the taut ropes linking the load to the crane. In post-war Britain taxes were introduced which were designed to discourage the domestic consumption of luxury goods such as motorcars so that they could be diverted to

Top: This magnificent picture depicts the arrival of an enormous Christmas tree at Grimsby Docks. It was the gift of the Scandinavian Butterboat Traders and represented an annual tradition. The word *magnificent* could also be used to describe the beautiful Shire horse and extended cart used to transport the tree to Riverhead (to a spot now occupied by the new bus shelters) whee it would be admired by Grimsby folk throughout the Christmas period.

Three lucky winners of a grand local raffle pose with their prizes early in the 1960s. All had paid a shilling each for the tickets, a wise investment for the ladies as things turned out. The first prize was a Lambretta 125cc scooter, freshly imported from Italy and a favourite mode of transport for every self-respecting 'Mod' (as opposed to their 'Rocker' counterparts). The lady standing behind the scooter looks less certain about the prospects of riding it than the organisers of the competition might have hoped. And who can blame her! The second prize was an English Electric 'Slimline 4' refrigerator - the object of many housewife's dreams in the early 1960s. Finally the third prize; a Hercules Balmoral cycle complete with dynamo and saddlebag and retailing for around £15 at this time.

Shopping spree

Below: The Yarborough Hotel towers over the damp canvass market stalls in this picture. People hurry for shelter and the market traders would have cursed the weather for the effect it was having on their takings. Still, this pair of passers-by took a moment or two to pose for a photographer despite the inclement conditions.

The young man in question is carrying an *Evening Telegraph* newspaper bag though we can't be sure if he was a paper boy or one of the town centre vendors. The photograph dates from the 1960s.

Right: An elevated view of the Old Market area, the whole scene dominated by a sea of canvass tent tops positioned over flimsy frames in order to protect stock from the elements. Market trading has been an important element of Grimsby life for many centuries and various markets have served the inhabitants of the town and surrounding countryside on different days of the week.

The Cattle Market - on Cromwell Road - was a centre of trading every Monday. Of course, the Corn Exchange played a vital role in the trade in farm and dairy produce, holding busy market days on Mondays and Fridays.

Other large open air markets were held in the Market Square on Tuesdays, Fridays and Saturdays.

NEL Museums

YOU TOO CAN BE DIFFERENT !

'You too can be different' proclaims the tiny sign in this ladies' outfitters shop. Not many Grimsby ladies would be prepared to look this different, despite their menfolk's interest in fish! The picture dates from the 1950s, a time when it was becoming possible to be more interested in fashion after the long war years and shortages which carried on afterwards. This delightful young lady had dressed in a mermaids' costume in order to publicise a fashion event at L & G Modes popular store in the Old Market Place. Some interesting details from the time can be seen on closer examination; the lady at the front of the group is wearing a fashionable hat with an enormous hat pin to keep it in place. Behind her a younger lady has a transparent plastic raincoat over her arm, a garment kept in the handbag of millions of women in case of unexpected downpours.

NEL Museums

Above: *Carefully arranged wooden shelves, purpose built in order to fit the small properties which had been converted into corner shops, remind us of being sent on shopping trips when young. As children we would wonder at the mysteries of the whirring bacon slicer and marvel at the skill of the grocer as he cut mouthwatering slices of cheese with a thin wire cutter. The chance of a 'treat' when the tight family budget allowed made a trip to the corner shop even more exciting. Enormous gob-stoppers, sherbets and penny-chews were familiar to all of us and sometimes a friendly grocer would give one to the children of his best customers as a special treat.*

Left: *Memories of shopping days in the old open-air market and surrounding shops are certain to be rekindled by this picture. This, the Old Market Place was the setting for those engaged in serious bargain-hunting. As children many of us will remember trips to the market with our mothers; the sights and sounds - let alone the distinctive aromas which wafted around the area, remained with us for many years.*

These were the days before everyone was obsessed with out of town shopping centres and concrete precincts full of well-known national shops.

As shopping habits changed there were implications for the shape of every town centre retail area and the phenomenon led to many buildings being reduced to rubble. Turners, on the left of the picture and Johnsons building on the right faced an uncertain future when this picture was taken. Johnsons was demolished in 1971. A solitary policeman looks in the direction of the photographer as he strolls around the market, arms behind his back, Dixon of Dock Green-style.

There would have been little to occupy the Bobby on his travels, other than the odd enquiry for directions or the tedium of endless point-duty. The scene appears very relaxed, indeed life in general seemed to be conducted at a slower pace altogether during the time depicted here.

The widespread introduction of traffic lights from the 1930s onwards was to free up the resources of many police forces from the burden of point-duty activities in our town centres.

At work

Below: This was the scene during the construction of the underpass destined to take traffic beneath the busy railway line along Weelsby Road. It dates from 1933. Leading up to this time the growth in the number of motor vehicles of all descriptions on Grimsby's roads had created a major and very frustrating bottleneck here. As traffic competed with the needs of rolling stock on the Louth to Grimsby rail route. The picture provides an interesting insight to the goings-on on a 1930s construction site. Most of the work relied on manpower, there being only limited forms of mechanical assistance available. Work outdoors was as arduous, as it is in many cases today, but in the troubled 1920s and '30s people were glad of any opportunity to earn their living.

Right: Ergo*whatics?* this photograph shows the interior of the Grimsby Telephone Exchange in an era when the study of how people should sit and work in their workplace 'ergonomics' had not quite filtered through to local managers! A variety of ladder-back and wheel-back chairs, more suitable for the dining room than the workplace were supplied for the almost exclusively female workforce. The Exchange itself was very labour-intensive there being up to eighty people at work in this room alone. The job was thought to be very suitable for young women. Friendships would begin among the girls here which would last lifetimes. Stern but generally kind hearted supervisors would enforce company rules concerning such things as the maximum number of times a receiver was allowed to ring before being answered. The photograph dates from the 1930s and it would be a long time before the female workers in Britain would get the same employment rights and opportunities as their male counterparts.

NEL Museums

Making the world a brighter place

For almost 50 years in Grimsby Tioxide's range of titanium dioxide pigments has been adding whiteness and brightness to a wide variety of end uses throughout the countries of the world.

Many of Tioxide's products add lustre to our everyday living, in house paint, in building products and industrial coatings. Tioxide whiteness is spread on a larger scale, over the world's tallest office blocks, famous cruisers and fleet aircraft of the largest international airlines. White and pastel shades of plastics used in most domestic appliances, toys and cables will almost certainly have been pigmented with high opacity titanium dioxide. Tioxide pigments add whiteness to writing paper, wallpaper, banknotes and postage stamps.

Titanium dioxide is non toxic and is completely safe for use in cosmetics, toiletries, food and food

packaging. It has almost entirely replaced older white pigments such as white lead and zinc oxide.

The Tioxide Group, whose founding name was British Titan Products, has been producing titanium dioxide since 1934 and now has

Above: Mrs Tasker, laying the foundation stone in May 1946.
Below: Staff posing for a photograph around the 1950's.

factories throughout the world, including two in Britain.

During the Second World War the Company started looking for a suitable site in the UK for a new plant. They needed a port at hand for shipment of raw materials, a plentiful supply of pure water, suitable building land, a residential area within easy reach, power supplies and a good turbulent river or estuary nearby for dispersion of the effluent. Grimsby was ideally suitable.

The Company was the first to buy land on the Grimsby Pyewipe where the then Borough Council owned about 200 acres, purchased from the estates of Sir Richard Sutton. In February 1945 the Company purchased 53 acres.

The sale was completed and construction work commenced on May 29th 1946 with the foundation stone

being laid by Mrs Tasker, wife of the Chairman at the time. The plant took nearly three years to complete and the factory was officially opened in July 1949 by HRH the Duke of Edinburgh. Production had begun in the previous January with an initial capacity of 10,000 tons per annum.

Above: Ladies hard at work typing.
Below: A smile from the ladies in the early days.

By 1960 the plant had expanded production to 60,000 tons a year. Expansion continued into the seventies until 1976 when production reached 100,000 tons a year. Even through the power crisis of 1973-74 the works managed to maintain an 80% capacity production.

When the recession started to bite, production was cut back and a period of rationalisation followed which continued until 1982 when the demand for titanium dioxide pigment began to rise again to the 1989 production figure of 105,000 tons a year.

Tioxide's Grimsby factory, known locally as "Titans", has expanded to become the largest in the Tioxide Group. It has now been a familiar part of the Grimsby skyline for nearly 50 years. In that time, continual and substantial investment has been made in plant, equipment, buildings and people.

Since it was built, the Grimsby factory has made a significant contribution to the local economy as a major employer in the area. The current workforce of four hundred is supported by around two hundred local contractors.

Above: Stacking them high, storing bags of pigment ready for distribution.
Below: Bags of pigment out of the warehouse and on their way to the customer.

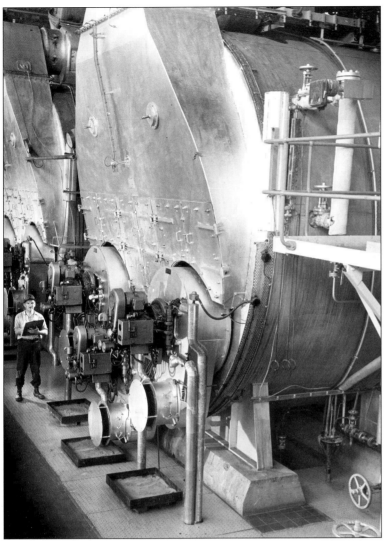

In addition, a "buy-local" policy ensures that local suppliers have also benefited.

From the earliest days the Company has been concerned about the environment, ensuring that the firm's operations are not causing problems. They monitor the air, estuarine water and sediments, and the animals that live there, for any possible effects. The results of these comprehensive monitoring exercises are sent to regulatory authorities and other bodies for their information and critical assessment.

Tioxide has a policy of 'environmental openness' which has produced some very positive results. Greenpeace has congratulated the Company for sitting in open forum with them and debating issues. There have been numerous consultation sessions with local councils to brief both politicians and their advisers prior to application for planning permission for environmental schemes.

Left: Staff monitoring the Boilerhouse.
Below: Lunch break "Tea up lads!".

7-8) the responsibility of banking the money and purchasing the necessary building materials as and when required whilst Tioxide employees constructed the feature.

Immingham children are delighted with the specially designed play park, climbing frame and slide which was designed, built and erected by Tioxide second year YTS employees.

A Tioxide Community Care Committee has been formed at Grimsby Works to ensure that

This open policy has helped to produce and maintain a good working relationship with the local press, with regular consultation on items of local interest.

requests for help and support are met from an annual budget. The budget is shared fairly

Above: A visit from the Duke of Edinburgh in 1949.
Below: A constructive working day.

Tioxide will continue to play a full and active role in safeguarding the Humber estuary by combining research and development with new techniques of environmental monitoring. They co-operate with all regulatory authorities and continue to take care of the local environment, its workforce and the local community.

Community care outside the Tioxide family involves literally dozens of initiatives and contributions to communities adjacent to Tioxide's sites. In Grimsby the Company has pioneered links with education and has developed many associations with local schools.

A redesigned mobile classroom at Wybers Wood First School is an ideal example of industry working with schools. A playground at Strand Street first School has been furnished with a play feature, which was designed by both the young pupils and Tioxide employees. In the latter example, Tioxide financially sponsored the exercise but gave the pupils (aged

within the local community with priority being given to schools and medical projects.

Tioxide's Grimsby Works has made significant and sound progress since the first production in 1949. All indications are that the Company will continue in this successful vein. A strong market demand promises to continue and Tioxide certainly plans to continue its capital investment and its involvement in a policy of improvement and change. Tioxide looks forward positively to the challenge of the advent of the twenty first century.

Above: Packers preparing new bags of pigment ready for dispatch.

Ice cold and freezer fresh

The success of Associated Cold Stores & Transport springs from an elegant solution to an age-old challenge.

Since time immemorial, man has struggled with the problem of keeping things (especially food) cool. The Ancient Egyptians and Indians exploited the effects of evaporation, whilst other cultures, notably the early Chinese and later the Greeks and Romans, stored natural ice and snow in underground pits to provide conditions suitable for cooling wine and other foodstuffs. From the late 18th century, the British adopted the technique of storing ice, hacked in winter from frozen lakes and ponds, in specially constructed 'ice houses'. Generally underground, these structures remained sufficiently cool, even in summer, to guarantee a permanent supply of ice and the first cold storage as we know it today.

In 1824, the first patents for 'freezing machines' began to appear. But it was a combination of factors at the end of the century that spawned dramatic developments in cooling technology. Change in tastes and the rise of an affluent middle class increased demand for meat. Domestic refrigeration became highly desirable - a market that could generally be satisfied - but the growing appetite for meat, and a shortage at home, led to supplies being sought from abroad. Australia and New Zealand, for their part, had surpluses - but how to transport it? The challenge was eventually surmounted in 1880 when the 'Strathleven' made the long voyage carrying a cargo of Australian meat which was satisfactorily chilled by a new Bell-Coleman machine using compressed air to achieve low temperatures. In 1890,

the first shipment of frozen meat arrived on our shores from New Zealand in a sailing ship, the 'Dunedin'. Marine refrigeration was born.

Associated Cold Stores and Transport, as we know it today, has its roots in the London Ice and Cold Storage Company. Established in 1921 by a cooperative of merchants at Billingsgate Market, London, to provide freezing and cold storage facilities for market surpluses, its major shareholders included W A Bennett, Sir (then Mr) David Robertson and the Bennett Companies (later to become Associated Fisheries). When the business prospered, the senior shareholders got together to establish Britain's first low temperature cold store on the Royal Dock in Grimsby. An initial capital investment of £25,000 was sufficient to generate profits that would later fund a massive programme of investment and expansion.

The new undertaking was named The Grimsby Cold Storage Company and began trading in 1934. Usefully located between the dock and a road and railway sidings, it represented the first commercial venture to promote brine freezing of whole fish as a solution to the perennial problem of preserving, on land, fish that had been trawled in distant waters. Under the scrupulous management of Mr Edwin Hart, who had for many years previously been manager of the Standard Ice Company, it was Grimsby's first public cold store, and the first in the country to offer storage at such low temperatures.

Above: A sea view of the warehouse in the early days, on the brink of prosperity.

Converted from its original purpose as a grain warehouse for the one-time Great Northern Railways (later LNER), the four-storey building had a capacity of 250,000 cubic feet and could immediately accommodate around 1,000 tons of fish, in particular halibut, which until then had to be stored, cold, in the holds of refrigerated ships that brought the catches into port. Although cold stores existed elsewhere in the country, they operated generally at temperatures between 16° and 20° F. The Grimsby Cold Storage Company, equipped with the first two-stage ammonia refrigerating compressors, was able to achieve far lower temperatures (essential for fish) and could also cater for the long term storage of bacon and butter - all carefully segregated, of course, to avoid the transmission of unwanted odours! The ground floor of the store comprised three separate chambers, one freezing at a steady 20°F, another for chilling at 26°F, and a third able to do either, according to demand. The first and second storeys, meanwhile, each held four chambers, heavily piped to maintain a temperature of 20°F. The wet quick-freezing brine tank, the principal attraction of the new store, could accommodate two tons of fish at any one time. An electric travelling crane lowered and lifted the fish to and from the tank by means of specially constructed galvanised metal trays and the sodium chloride brine, maintained at a steady -4.5°F, circulated around the fish during the freezing process. This pioneering technique was an instant success. 'Fish' said the July 1934 editorial of Cold Storage Review, 'treated in this tank have exceeded all expectations, having a better texture, taste and appearance than slowly-frozen fish.'

The store's refrigerating machinery, all installed by Messrs L Sterne & Co of Glasgow and London,

Above: Billingsgate fish market, London.
Below: No 9 Cold Store, Grimsby Docks.

large accumulator and an innovative two-stage centrifugal pump was connected between the accumulator and the expansion valve header. The Grimsby Cold Storage store was the first to boast this advanced technology - and it was quick to prove its worth.

Demand for the store's facilities was so great that, within weeks, the remaining two storeys were being converted to increase capacity - establishing a pattern that has continued throughout the company's history. By 1949, and the development of further premises at the dock, a further 400,000 cubic feet had been

consisted of three two-stage compressors, direct-coupled to electric motors. It was already well-known that the efficiency of the more common single-stage compressors fell off rapidly as suction pressure was lowered (necessary for achieving really low temperatures), and Sterne & Co had developed their two-stage compressors to tackle this problem and to meet market demand for machines that were efficient at low-evaporating temperatures. At the new store, the condensers were of the 'block' type and were situated outside the engine room - condensing water was pumped directly from the dock. The direct expansion coils and brine evaporator operated on the flooded ammonia system, while a float valve automatically controlled the supply of liquid to a

added, by 1957 an additional 700,000. Apart from a brief spell in the recession-hit seventies, rapid expansion followed to provide, by 1986, a total volume 8.3 million cubic feet, over eight different stores, in Grimsby alone.

The outbreak of war in 1939 applied brakes on the Company's ambitious expansion plans and the cold store was, for a time, given over to the Ministry of Food; but as the Fish Docks sprang into life again, after 1945, business was soon booming. In 1952, Mr Hart retired as

Above: No 6 Cold Store, Grimsby.
Below: Staff posing for their photograph around the 1970s and ready for distributing frozen food.

manager and was succeeded by Mr Frank Croft - a popular figure, who presided over a period of great advancement for the Company. The increased demand for freezing and storage facilities saw the installation, in 1953, of two Williams plate-freezers, and diversification in the range of fish handled. Quick-freezing of smaller fish, such as sprats and herring, for the canning industry was soon paving the way for yet more versatility. Indeed, it is the Company's proud claim to have been the first in this country to freeze peas. An interesting fact for those of us who would find life unimaginable without them!

By the mid-1950s, the volume of business being generated locally led to the acquisition, in 1955, of a third set of premises off the dock in Robinson Street. Equipped with a blast freezer, there was room here for 350,000 cubic feet of cold store. But the dramatic rise of the quick-frozen industry soon forced more development and in 1958 the Company's fourth cold store opened on the dock, marking a new era in storage techniques. Consisting of two chambers, with a capacity of 420,000 cubic feet, it was the company's first fully palletised store - allowing three or four standard 48" x 40" pallets to be stacked to a height of 20 feet by fork-lift trucks.

In 1959, following the death of W A Bennett, the entire business (including the parent company of London Cold Storage) was acquired by Associated Fisheries, who were keen to take advantage of a growing market not only for frozen fish, but for frozen food in general. The programme of expansion continued apace. In 1961, the company opened yet another cold store on the dock side. Dedicated exclusively to quick-frozen foods, and with a staggering 710,000 cubic feet of storage in a single chamber, the new store was soon housing 450 separate varieties of frozen foods in huge quantities.

1968 saw the company embarking on a completely new venture with the construction of a freezing plant and cold store on a green field site at Tewkesbury. The principal aim of this development was to offer facilities to the fruit trade, and its choice of location came only after extensive research in the West Midlands area. True to the company's form, it was quickly a success and has itself seen a programme of expansion in subsequent years - to over 3.6 million cubic feet of capacity and the provision of many ancillary services.

In March 1970, the company extended its operation in the West Midlands region through the purchase of the Government Cold Store in Wolverhampton, previously operated by the Ministry of Agriculture, Fisheries and Food. At the time of the acquisition, Cadbury's was already a significant customer, storing chocolate for the Christmas and Easter trades. Confectionery remains a staple at the store, but has been joined by, amongst other things, meat and dairy products. Storage capacity has increased greatly since the company took it over.

Over the years, and in contrast to the early days when an emphasis on halibut, butter and bacon prevailed, the company has seen a vast array of produce passing through its stores: imported frozen meat and lamb, ice cream, soft fruits, vegetables from the rich agricultural fields of Lincolnshire and fish from all over the globe, including hake from South Africa, prawns from Japan and much else besides from countries as far apart as Canada, Norway, and New Zealand. A significant proportion of the business was devoted to a growing pet food industry. In less enlightened times, whalemeat was commonly used by manufacturers in dog- and cat-food products, and the company stored large quantities of it - in 28lb blocks - after its arrival in Grimsby or Immingham from the whaling nations of Japan, Iceland and Norway. Strangest of all, perhaps, were two baby

Above: The Cold Store stacked full of frozen food.

Steady, but somewhat slow, expansion of the business had followed, but was accelerated rapidly after it came under the control of Associated Fisheries, providing refrigerated equipment for Bird's Eye, Findus, and Caterpac (McCain) in Grimsby and for Bird's Eye in Lowestoft. In 1970, it acquired McVeigh Transport Ltd and advertising produced soon afterwards demonstrates that at this time the business operated some 500 vehicles and 1100 trailers from 22 depots scattered all over the country. Over the next few years, bases were opened in Scarborough, to service McCain's requirements, and also at Honey Pot Lane, Colsterworth for the benefit of Pellew Harvey. However, the troubled economic climate of the 1970s, coupled with significant industrial decline, had a marked effect - and the decade was distinctive as a time of severe rationalisation, with the closure of non-profit making depots and a contraction in operating fleets. By 1980, the business had been streamlined into just four depots from the original 22, at Grimsby, Immingham, Seamer and Colsterworth. Of these, Seamer Transport and Granton Transport were operating refrigerated fleets, Immingham a general goods fleet, and Grimsby some of each.

whales who had been caught by the Faroese factory ship 'Caribia'. Destined originally for Flamingo Park Zoo in North Yorkshire, they sadly died before reaching the shore but, at the request of the London Hospital Medical College, were frozen at sea before being landed at Grimsby. Grimsby Cold Storage were happy to provide free storage for the animals until the College was able to transport them to London for the purpose of medical research. Fortunately, the service has never been required again.

One of the most difficult products in the companies vast experience has been quick- frozen poultry. Chickens are a notoriously difficult foodstuff to store economically - not only because of the enormous range of weights and sizes, but more particularly because of their extremely awkward shape, especially in palletised stores where a good deal of space is already taken up with alleyways and the pallets themselves. It is, however, a character-istic of the company to meet these challenges head on, and a testament to management and staff alike that imaginative solutions, and effective working routines have earned the business a cast-iron reputation for reliable efficiency.

In keeping with Associated Fisheries' broadening activ-ities, a transport and warehousing division was estab-lished in 1965 through the acquisition of Humber Warehousing - a business which had its origins in Lincoln but in the late 1950s transferred its transport operations to Grimsby where it specialised in providing refrigerated transport for the growing number of frozen food companies such as Bird's Eye, Ross and Findus.

At a meeting in Queen Anne's Gate, London on 22 May 1984, it was formally agreed that the Transport and Cold Storage Divisions of Associated Fisheries should be combined and, in consequence, should henceforward be known as Associated Cold Stores and Transport Ltd. A single management team was created and led by Mr David Nurse who was appointed Managing Director. One of the principal objectives for the new concern was to develop its twin areas of expertise - cold storage and transportation - to establish a national distribution service for frozen foods. Associated Fisheries invested £8.5 million, and saw their confidence rewarded when the objective was realised in a few short years.

Above: Dates back to 1968 when Associated Fisheries Companies bought nearly 2,300 Kits which is equivalent to about three quarter million fish meals.

Associated Cold Stores & Transport Limited continue go from strength to strength. If it's in your freezer, they've probably handled it! From a relatively modest start in a converted dock-side warehouse they have today become a world-famous frozen force to be reckoned with.

Associated Cold Stores & Transport Limited is renowned as a well established and successful supplier of storage, order assembly and distribution services to the frozen food industry.

Ironically, one of the prime reasons for its reputation for stability and reliability is its enthusiasm in embracing new ideas to enhance its traditional services.

As a constant feature of its "business plan", ACS&T is committed to the continuous review and planned modification of systems to provide its customers with the most efficient temperature controlled storage and distribution service.

They have installed a warehouse management system in all of their fifteen cold stores to record and control the flow of product from manufacturer to delivery point.

They are engaged on a programme to convert their distribution cold stores to become paperless by the introduction of Belgravium radio data terminals, for each operative to communicate with the computer base.

Already half of the fleet of temperature controlled vehicles has been supplied with surveillance equipment to maintain a constant central check on temperatures and associated matters from hundreds of miles away and thereby protect the integrity of customers product.

Currently they are establishing a customer stock enquiry service through the Internet system, actively encouraging existing and new customers to have a two-way computer link with them for transferring all operational and management information.

Recently, they qualified as an Investor in People and ensure that their staff is trained to keep pace with technological development.

All of these facilities, and more, are under scrutiny and they shall improve them, or replace them, as and when technology advances sufficiently to provide them with a superior alternative.

Associated Cold Stores & Transport Limited are at the forefront of modern communication and its application and they intend to remain there.

Their record of achievement in this area reflects this attitude and endeavour.

Above: An aerial view of the head office site in Grimsby in 1970.
Right: Mr Nurse with other members of the board of directors escorting the Right Honourable Michael Joplin who was the Minister of Agriculture, Fisheries and Food on the occasion of the opening of stage 5 Cold Store, Grimsby in December 1986.

Going Dutch - The story of SSM Coal

SSM Coal at Immingham Dock is part of a multi-national concern whose roots are nourished, indeed were planted, across the North Sea in the coal-free territory of the Netherlands.

In 1896, the Dutch were wholly dependent for their energy supplies on a mighty German coal syndicate who exercised a virtual monopoly over Westphalia's vast bunker coal reserves, and who exported to a wide range of countries unable to support rapid industrialisation with their own fuel stocks. By contrast, Britain - the very instigator of the Industrial Revolution - was blessed with an abundance of fossil fuel riches. When SHV ('Steenkolen Handelsvereeniging' - or the Coal Trading Association) which was a shipping and haulage company, won exclusive import rights in Holland for the German coal. The American Petroleum Company immediately established a rival in Rotterdam (afterwards owned by Rotterdam businessman Willem van de Vorm.) Named Scheepvaart en Steenkolen Maatschappij, or SSM for short, it was to achieve early success by importing British coal in direct competition with SHV.

The British grade of bunker coal was soon in great demand - SSM opened branches across Holland as its customer base grew, and soon had offices in the UK - in Newcastle, Hull and Glasgow - to support its operation. Before the outbreak of the First World War in 1914, SSM set up a wholly-owned British subsidiary, the London-based Shipping & Coal Company Ltd, with Mr van de Vorm at the helm, to look after the UK side of the business. A chain of regional offices were rapidly set in place. Immingham, ideally placed on the sea route to Holland, had its first SSM office as early as 1913, and Grimsby Docks soon followed as a vital link between England's hugely productive coal fields and their new Dutch customers. Importing and exporting remained the core activity of the young company, but a characteristic verve ensured there was early diversification too - coal distribution became a profitable sideline, while its coal transportation activities achieved early renown. Marine transport technology was in its infancy - and SSM showed the way with pioneering sea-going lighters carrying huge quantities of coal in convoy, towed by a fully-laden collier. Before long, vessels that began sailing empty across the North Sea to take on loads of British coal, were laden with general cargo from Holland - especially cement, pitch and gas - finding ready markets in the UK.

Top: Trucks loaded with sacks of of coal in Amsterdamn, 1924. Below left: Minutes from 29th May 1940. Below: Exporting to Germany in the early days.

century, SSM had become a truly global concern, with a branch network that stretched from New York to Maastricht, from Buenos Aires to Copenhagen.

The British operation, meanwhile, was struggling to keep up. By the mid-1960s our domestic coal supplies were proving too expensive for foreign markets. The dawn of the industrialised world's love affair with oil had begun, and coal-producers world-wide could hold their own only by savage price cutting. Poland, the Soviet Union and even Germany pursued this path, while Britain lost her footing. The discovery of our own North Sea Oil cushioned the blow, but UK coal became uncompetitive elsewhere. SSM simply ceased to regard this country as a major supplier. A period of limbo followed through the 1970s and early 1980s, culminating in the massive pit closure programme of more recent years. The Immingham branch of SSM closed during this time, and a tragic irony emerged. Britain - the source of all SSM's early success - specialised for more of the upper markets. We needed to look abroad for supplies, and SSM was supremely placed to assist.

There was no mistaking it. SSM had swiftly asserted itself as a formidable rival to SHV - and was so effective that even the Westphalian coal cartel began to crumble! The company capitalised on its success and set up a subsidiary in Germany itself - selling British coal at the hearth, as it were, of the commercial enemy.

In 1914, of course, Germany became a real enemy - and a period of genuine difficulty afflicted SSM. Export markets in Germany and Belgium vanished under the mud of trench warfare, and a host of company vessels were lost at sea. A resilient fight-back, after the war was over, saw a New York office open in 1920, and 1.5 million tonnes of USA coal imported in its first year; but then came turbulent social unrest in Europe, typified by the British General Strike in 1926 - the first time in history that Newcastle had to import coal. Again SSM responded - developing new sources of supply in Germany, Belgium and now Poland too.

By the outbreak of the Second World War, SSM had fashioned its distinctive business approach - innovative, keenly responsive to fluctuating demands, confident in penetrating new markets, and highly adaptable in a world of convulsive political change. In under half a

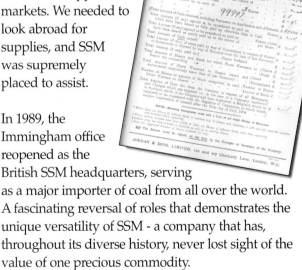

In 1989, the Immingham office reopened as the British SSM headquarters, serving as a major importer of coal from all over the world. A fascinating reversal of roles that demonstrates the unique versatility of SSM - a company that has, throughout its diverse history, never lost sight of the value of one precious commodity.

Top: A mozaic showing SSM Coal vessels. The mozaic was done in 1921 celebrating SSM being in business for twenty five years.
Right: Dated 9th May 1914 this page shows the summary of share capital and figures.
Left: SSM's colliers and bunkering equipment.

Building to last

They have long been builders. Brick dust must be in the blood. James Bratton started as an apprentice bricklayer working alongside his father, George and as his building skills grew, so did an ambition one day to run his own Company. It was some years, however, before his dream could be realised. The political and economic crises of the 1920s (including the General Strike in 1926) were followed rapidly by a deep Depression in the early1930s. But in 1934, James had a stroke of luck. Mr E A H Jennison and his son Mr S F Jennison agreed to provide supporting financial backing to enable James to form his own limited Company. So it was that on 11 May 1934 James Bratton and Co Ltd was born.

The business began its operation from a loft and store at the rear of Cartergate in the back garden of Mr. S.F. Jennison's house, 4 Dudley Street, Grimsby. James Bratton started at the helm as Managing Director and remained there without interruption until his death in April 1976. In its first year of trading, James Bratton and Co achieved a turnover of £7,294. From the earliest days the company set out to gain a reputation for quality of workmanship and service which would stand the test of time. It worked and in a few short years they were able to move to larger premises in Cromwell Road, just before the outbreak of the Second World War.

The War brought its own problems for the now fully-fledged business. During the 1930s, labour had been cheap and easy to come by (unemployment stood at nearly three million in 1933, and at just under two million in 1938), but with the introduction of compulsory military service in June 1939 there was a sudden, and acute, shortage of men. James Bratton rose to the challenge and the Company survived. In 1940 he was able to take his business to London to play his part in the massive clear-up operation after the Blitz.

In 1947, Mr Raymond Roe joined the Company as an apprentice joiner and, apart from two years National Service, spent all his working life there, rising through the ranks to become site agent in 1957, Contracts Manager in 1965 before being appointed a Director in 1971 and remaining until his retirement in 1989. The late Mr William Butler, also appointed a director in 1971, had spent over twelve years beforehand dealing with estimating, planning, contract supervision etc before he too retired in 1990. It is this kind of life-long attachment

Above: James Bratton, founder of the company which dates back to 1934. Left: The original ledger showing the first profit and loss account. Below: James Bratton in his early twenties working as a builder, learning his trade.

offer an unrivalled service to its clients, delivering a quality and range of expertise that has won widespread acclaim. Projects are varied, embracing much commercial and local authority work - housing developments by James Bratton & Co can be seen all over the region, not only in Grimsby - and pub refurbishment is a particular speciality, where the joiners' workshop really comes into its own!

which typifies the Company's closely knit family atmosphere and outlook. So it is all the more appropriate that James Bratton's son Nigel (a Chartered Accountant by profession) should have joined the firm as Financial Director in 1973, succeeded his father as Managing Director in 1976 and now runs the business together with his wife Jacqueline (the Company Secretary) and John Stanley who commenced with the firm in 1974 having earlier served his apprenticeship with Hewins & Goodhand Ltd (another byword for the Grimsby building trade) and whom had been established a lot longer even than James Bratton & Co.

In 1984, James Bratton & Co celebrated their Golden Jubilee able to boast an annual turnover of over £1 million. A celebration luncheon marked the occasion, attended by the Worshipful Mayor of Great Grimsby, Councillor Tony Rouse.

These days the Company is based at Alexandra Road, in premises acquired in 1968. As one of the few building Companies to retain its own joiners' workshop, it is able to

One of the Company's most interesting contracts reached completion in Louth in November 1997 when 'The Bishop raised his staff and smote three times on the door of the new Holy Trinity Church Centre'. The church in Louth had been burnt out in 1991, leaving little more than the tower still standing, and its congregation homeless. James Bratton & Co worked painstakingly to realise its modern replacement, designed by architect Sebastian Rowe (of the Hill Rowe Partnership, Ripon). Conceived in brick, to reflect local building materials as well as for budgetary reasons, the new structure incorporates modern amenities within an inspirational scheme of interlocking octagons which in turn reflect the octagonal top of the surviving Victorian tower. It is, in short, a celebration of old and new coming together - a gesture of serene hope for the future steadied on the firm foundations of the past. A project of which James Bratton would heartily approve.

Top left: Holy Trinity Church, Louth .
Above: One of the very first business cards of James Bratton.
Left: From left to right John Stanley, Jacqueline and Nigel Bratton, and inset Charles Bratton (non executive director).

The Sea's Worth

In 1862 there arrived in Grimsby a new shipping agent, sent at the behest of the Manchester, Sheffield and Lincolnshire Railway to work on behalf of the recently formed Anglo French Steamship Company. A man of 49 years, and originally from Rochdale, he had spent all his working life in the thick of that most 19th century of obsessions - transport. His new role in Grimsby was to herald the birth of the long standing shipping company we know today as John Sutcliffe & Son.

John Sutcliffe, they say, had a voice like a fog horn - audible from one side of a dock to the other. His arrival in Grimsby coincided with the town's most rapid expansion in its history, and he was clearly ready to make his mark. In June 1862, John Sutcliffe and Company was established in Royal Dock Chambers. Almost immediately, he acquired a prestigious residence - Stallingborough Manor, some six miles West of the town. It was a wise move - he and his wife, Isabela, already had five children, and three more were to follow - but it also demonstrates that John Sutcliffe was setting about that most Victorian of activities: founding a dynasty.

The early business of the company was devoted to Anglo French's trade - in return for which Sutcliffe received 5% of all freight on the Grimsby to Hamburg route. But in time the new firm diversified to become general commission agents and shipbrokers to a widening group of clients. Just under 1500 vessels from foreign ports were visiting Grimsby in 1864, handling cargoes as diverse as coal, timber, agricultural machinery and raw cotton. When Anglo French was dissolved in 1865, John Sutcliffe was enviably placed to take advantage of what had become the fifth ranking port in the UK. He worked hard to develop new trades, including the importation of manufactured goods from the Continent for reshipment in Liverpool, and successfully saw off competition from Hull in retaining for Grimsby the shipping interests of the Manchester, Sheffield and Lincolnshire Railway. It was not only his firm which was to prosper, but - through his endeavours - the port of Grimsby as a whole. By 1870, eleven thousand vessels - carrying 837,887 tons of goods - were using the port.

John Sutcliffe's son Jack joined him in the Agency at the age of eighteen in 1863. His father was adamant that he should learn the business by working up from the bottom and Jack was soon gaining first hand experience in every aspect of the trade. His natural aptitude reaped swift rewards: he was made a full partner in 1872, at the age of 27. Thereafter the firm traded as John Sutcliffe & Son. With his financial future assured, Jack married Harriet Garvey a year later. The couple set up home in Field House, Bargate where they were to spend forty

Above: John Sutcliffe founded the company in 1862.
Below: The Sutcliffe Anniversary Group with Jack Sutcliffe seated in the centre.

happy years and bring up five children.
When John Sutcliffe died in 1877 he left his son at the helm of a thriving enterprise. Jack enthusiastically moved the firm forward, assisted by his brothers Harry and Tom. Expansion was the order of the day, both for the company and for the port as a whole. It was at this period that fish dock provision came into its own at Grimsby. By the turn of the century it was to reach fame as the largest fishing port in the world. Jack even moved into ship ownership himself, buying the iron steamship Zulu in 1879, quickly followed by a series of successful sailing craft.

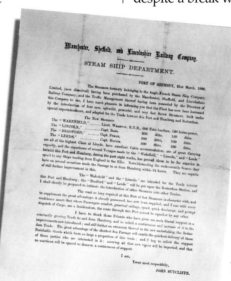

When he died in 1913, his funeral was attended by a vast number of mourners, flags flew at half mast and the tributes came thick and fast. 'Alderman Sutcliffe' wrote one 'was a very sunny man, always ready to encourage anything that increased the joy of life...respected not only by his own staff, but by every labourer on the docks.'

His son Ernest assumed the reins and successfully steered the company through the dark days of the First World War (when every Sutcliffe ship was lost), the General Strike of 1926, the collapse of the German currency and much else besides. It was always his belief that these storms could be weathered - and his resilience inspired his staff and persuaded his clients to retain their allegiance.

In 1936, Sutcliffe & Son became two companies - John Sutcliffe & Son (Grimsby) Ltd - acting as liner agents and stevedores - and John Sutcliffe & Son (Agencies) Ltd - procuring cargoes from the Midlands and forming a liaison between the shippers, or receivers, and the Port Offices.

Ernest's private interests, perhaps understandably, were more tranquil: his family, his home (Stewton House in

Louth), the breeding of dogs, and his beloved garden brimming with exotic plants. His son Peter joined the company after National Service in 1947 and, in time-honoured fashion, worked his way through each department with such alacrity that he was made a Director in September 1948.

Indeed, by the time of his father's death in 1951 he was already effectively leading the business, which had extensive ships agency, transport and warehousing operations throughout the U.K. at a time when the shipping industry was radically changing with the introduction of container operations and roll-on/roll-off ferries.

His son, James, after a period of working in Scandinavia and South America, joined the board in 1980 and, despite a break with tradition when Peter fully retired in 1986 and Christopher Thompson chaired the company for a short period, James bought out the minority shareholders in 1987 and took over the Group as the 5th generation Chairman.

Since then the company has prospered, with its strategy to consolidate at Grimsby and on the east coast of the U.K., privatising the Port of Boston in 1990 and developing a new joint venture stevedoring company, an insurance broking business, and a Colchester office handling services to the Middle East. John Sutcliffe sold their interests in the Port of Boston to The Cleveland Trust Plc, in 1997 but continue to manage the port. After 135 years in Grimsby, the company has purchased a new head office, which underwrites the company's long term commitment to the port and town of Grimsby.

Top left: Jack Sutcliffe in 1910 on one of his vessels.
Above: A document from John Sutcliffe to the Steam Ship Department from 1866.
Below: A Sutcliffe agency vessel in Grimsby today.

GPE - Pipework for ship and shore

Grimsby Pipework and Engineering Limited is today devoted to the provision of expert manufacturing, construction and maintenance services to the Humberbank industries. But its location in Murray Street, on the Fish Docks, gives a clue to its interesting origins.

In 1907, a group of trawler owners formed a consortium to establish facilities for the repair and maintenance of plumbing systems on steam trawlers and merchant ships. Named the Grimsby Plumbing Company, the enterprise found its first home in a corrugated iron shack, right on the Fish Docks. The Port of Grimsby - then the largest fishing port in the world - was at its height and business was brisk. When the First World War broke out, the Admiralty was quick to enlist the Company's skills and workforce for the vital task of keeping minesweepers and other warships in a good state of repair. By the end of the war in 1918, the company was able to move to larger premises in Robinson Lane, and, although things have expanded a good deal since those early days - with the addition of myriad workshops and an office block - it remains there to this day.

But how is it that a small marine plumbing business should have, in the course of ninety years, become the specialist force that is GPE today? The answer lies in the changing fortunes of Grimsby itself.

The Port of Grimsby owed its early success to the industrial revolution and the sudden prominence of markets, both at home and abroad, for coal and heavy goods

associated with the new manufacturing age. The 'black gold' of the South Yorkshire coal field found a ready route, thanks to a burgeoning railway system, to foreign customers like Holland through the East coast port. By the end of the nineteenth century, however, Grimsby had become synonymous with fish, and the establishment of dedicated Fish Docks ensured its future for almost a century. GPE's early days were spent at the heart of this legendary trade, fitting out trawlers with everything from pipework to ship's kettles. As late as 1970, this work accounted for nearly three quarters of the firm's turnover. And then, disaster struck in the form of fishing quotas and the Cod War. It has been

Above: Harry Chatterton presented with an award for 55 of service.
Below: Managing Director, Mr Jones and Finance Director Mr Powers, celebrating with some of the management and workers.

argued that the fishing industry was already in decline, and much made of the changing habits in meat and fish consumption following the end of the Second World War, but there can be no doubt that the sudden, and unilateral, extension of fishing limits around the coasts of Norway and Iceland - to encompass waters traditionally trawled by British vessels - was to have catastrophic consequences for Grimsby's staple industry.

Grimsby Plumbing Company was taken over by the Ross Group in 1950 at a time of great optimism for the Port's future. When the impact of the Scandinavian dispute began to make itself felt, however, the firm's management were swift to see compelling arguments for generating new markets. The decline in fishing at Grimsby had been accompanied by a steady development of factories along the Humber Bank - and it was to these that the company now turned for business. Pipefitters and welders joined the plumbers, and contracts with Conoco Courtuaulds and Norsk Hydro swiftly followed. In 1975, this change of direction was consolidated by a £750,000 contract for work at Ciba Geigy, prompting a change of company name to the more appropriate Grimsby Pipework & Engineering.

A period of expansion followed - and changes in ownership as the business redefined its role. In 1985 it was in the control of Celtic Haven, subsequently a part of West Industries; then, seven years later GPE found itself in the unenviable position of being a profitable asset to a parent company going into receivership. The two directors - Bob Jones and Jim Powers - stepped in to purchase the Company, and with the help of local accountants and solicitors, together with the support of the management and workforce secured the future of the company.

Nowadays, GPE's activities are diverse - fabrication, installation and maintenance work is undertaken across a broad spectrum of industries - food, textile, chemical, synthetic rubber, pharmaceutical, and oil companies have all benefited from GPE's expertise, and the business now has an undisputed reputation for high-level contract fulfilment across a wide range of requirements: from repairs to the Severn Bridge to fire-fighting equipment for the Middle East.

In 1997 Jim Powers sold his share of the company to L.E.S. Engineering Ltd another large and progressive company in Grimsby. The two companies complement each other and together offer a complete engineering solution, which will service the needs of the local industries well into the new millennium.

A far cry from the old shack on the fish docks - but a supreme example of how one business has been able to weather the storms of a turbulent century.

Above: *Pipework and plant fabricated and installed at Novartis.*
Left: *An absorber Tower being loaded onto a low loader outside the workshop in 1986.*

Simon Storage Immingham Terminals

The Immingham Storage Company's tank farms and associated facilities occupy the Humber Bank areas on each side of the entrance to Immingham Dock.

Some of the storage tanks are located at the exact site from which the Pilgrim Fathers left these shores in the early part of the 17th Century en route to practice their religious freedom in Holland and eventually in America.

Immingham Storage Company is now a part of the Simon Storage Group which is jointly owned by Simon Group and Van Ommeren, a Dutch company with major worldwide shipping and storage operations.

Simon Storage also operates terminals on other major estuaries throughout the United Kingdom and in Ireland.

The company commenced trading in 1929, thus being one of the longest established businesses in the area.

Initially, the primary objective was to provide storage tanks for creosote, a by-product of coal gas production, which was exported to the United States for use as timber preservative and also for the treatment of wooden pit props for UK coal mines.

After the first tank was built in 1929, growth in the 1930's was limited to new tanks for molasses (processed

from Lincolnshire sugarbeet and then exported from Immingham) and also storage for ships bunkering fuel.

The Immingham Storage Company terminals are well placed geographically to serve the major centres of the UK chemical industry which are situated along the M62 corridor and the markets of the North and Midlands.

Connections are made by road, rail, pipeline, sea, river and canal. Immingham is ideally located to access the massive oil and chemical trade which is centred on Rotterdam.

It was only after the 1939-1945 War, and in particular during the first part of the 1960's, that the emphasis shifted sharply away from handling tar based products such as creosote, no longer available due to the closure of coke fired gas works, to storing hydrocarbon fuels based on oil and gas. Between 1961-1964 the west side terminal tank farm expanded from six tanks, storing a total of twelve thousand cubic metres, to eighty five smaller tanks containing ten times as much fuel.

Development spread to include the east side of Immingham Dock in 1964 and both sites continued to grow. By the nineties the teminals had grown to two hundred and sixty tanks, some of which hold fifteen thousand cubic metres each, with a total capacity of five hundred and eighty thousand cubic metres.

Immingham Storage Company is the largest independent bulk liquid storage terminal in the UK.

Above: An aerial view of Immingham Storage in 1960.
Left: A tanker discharging oil on the Western Jetty.

Recently, the emphasis has changed towards more specialised facilities which are necessary to correctly handle the wide range of materials which are currently stored. In addition to the traditional carbon steel storage tanks, the range of facilities now includes specialist units such as stainless steel construction, Special protective linings and pressure vessels for liquid gases.

ISCo's overall capacity was more than doubled between 1965 and 1975 to provide storage for "new entrant" oil companies. These had expanded into the British market on the tide of fresh supplies of crude oil from oil fields being developed in North Africa.

Since the mid-70's the emphasis has moved from handling mineral oil to storing chemicals and other specialist products such as liquid gases and materials' requiring stainless steel containers. Some older, larger tanks have been dismantled to provide space for more specialised facilities. Many others at the Killingholme site have been converted into "dry product" warehouses for agricultural fertiliser and general cargo. A large open space in the centre of the west side terminal was once occupied by the power house which operated the immense dock gates. ISCo acquired the site in the early eighties and it has now been developed as a modern loading area.

Immingham Storage Company's emphasis on safety has resulted in the achievement of a number of RoSPA Gold Awards in recent successive years. Similarly, the Company was amongst the first in the industry to become accredited under the ISO 9002 system for quality assurance. The company remains at the forefront of this sector of UK industry.

Above left: A view of some of the tanks.
Above: An aerial view of the terminal today.
Below: How the company looks today with tank storage and automatic road loading systems.

Almost a hundred years of practising law for Wilkin Chapman

In 1897, at the age of 25, Mr Ben Chapman - a local man - established himself as a solicitor in Grimsby. We know from an old copy of the Grimsby News that in the same year another solicitor, Mr James Whiteley Wilkin, was practising at 47 Victoria Street. How these two men came together is a matter lost to history, but in 1900 they established a professional partnership that has, over the ensuing century, grown and matured into the formidable team, comprising some 150 partners and staff working in seven centres, that is Wilkin Chapman as we know it today.

The work of a provincial solicitors' office at the start of the century was very different from that now undertaken by the complex, multi-speciality practices of modern times. Family Law was virtually non-existent - divorce a rarity, the custody of children seldom an issue of official dispute - Legal Aid not yet even a gleam in the legislator's eye, whilst Commercial matters commonly involved little more than straightforward contracts and businesses - a far cry from the complex ownership structures of today - were generally family affairs, passing from father to son as a matter of course. Messrs Wilkin and Chapman concentrated then on conveyancing and probate and trust with services to local businesses and a small amount of litigation thrown in for good measure.

Above left: James Whiteley Wilkin.
Right: Ben Chapman, both Mr Wilkin and Mr Chapman are the founders of the firm.
Below: Partners and Staff at a dinner and dance in 1959 at the Royal Hotel.

The early years were spent at Victoria Street, in Mr Wilkin's former office. It is not clear how long this arrangement lasted, but certainly by 1914, and the outbreak of the First World War, the gentlemen had moved next door into the Prudential Chambers (over what is now Abbey National). This remained the firm's home until 1958, when it moved to its current premises in New Oxford House.

While it would be fanciful to suggest that the personal service offered today by Wilkin Chapman in any way resembles the Victorian version of its founders, it is at least true that both have been entirely fitting for their times. The changes wrought over the years reflect dramatic developments not only in the legal profession itself, but in society at large, and the firm has responded vigorously to them all.

1949 saw the introduction of Legal Aid and a rapid expansion in the demand for family and litigation services. The firm swiftly developed its expertise in these areas and in the same year opened a second office in Cleethorpes. Other branches were to follow: Immingham in 1967, Louth in 1981, Horncastle in 1992 and Lincoln in 1998. Also in 1992, a dedicated Family Law Centre was established next to the courts in Grimsby. Each office team is tailored to the needs of its locality, so, for example, Louth and Horncastle demonstrate a particular emphasis on agricultural law, trust and taxation to reflect their rural settings, as well as serving the rest of the community - including businesses, private and legally aided clients.

During the 1960s, the firm's Commercial Department began a period of significant growth in response to the needs of a large client, the Ross Group. This process has continued unabated as economic activity has mushroomed in the region - particularly on the Humber Bank - and the improvement in transport and other communication facilities have enabled Wilkin Chapman to extend their client base to include businesses throughout the United Kingdom.

The firm now offers specialists and departments in a wide range of fields, including employment, personal injury, debt, and professional negligence, as well as probate, agricultural and family services. A kaleidoscope of activity next to the firm's original focus on domestic property (a market now in decline)!

At the heart of all this high-powered diversity, lies a cogent philosophy: to offer the very best in client care, whatever needs are presented, at a reasonable price. An ongoing relationship with clients ensures that feedback on the firm's service is regularly sought and acted on. In all respects, it is an enterprise that puts people first. The Wilkin Chapman team is just that: a team - working together in a spirit of cooperation to achieve common goals. Hardly surprising, therefore, that in 1995 they were awarded the Investor in People Standard.

In 1999 the Cleethorpes office will be celebrating its 50th anniversary, to be marked throughout the year by a varied programme of events and activities. 2000, meanwhile, will see Wilkin Chapman's biggest landmark so far - its own centenary.

Above: A close up view of company premises in the evening.

Harry Carr Ltd - fiftieth anniversary

Harry Carr Limited, the electrical and mechanical building services specialist, owes its existence to the vision and determination of one man, whose name the company still bears.

Born in 1901, Harry Carr left school to take up an electrician's apprenticeship in the early years of this century. During the First World War, he worked on the Humber River Forts and subsequently worked his way up through the industry to become a foreman electrician.

In 1941 an opportunity rose for Harry, J A Sills and S A Sills, a father and son team of building contractors who operated from a yard in Wellowgate agreed to go into partnership with Harry in what was for them a new venture: electrical and refrigeration. The death of J.A. Sills in 1945 heralded the end of the partnership and by 1949 Harry Carr was able to establish the concern as a Limited Company. Within a short time, the business acquired its own premises at 7 West St Mary's Gate and Somersby Street, Grimsby. The company moved to its current, purpose-built headquarters, in Armstrong Street in 1973.

Even in the early days, the hallmarks of Harry Carr Limited were distinctive - a commitment to unrivalled technical skill, an insistence on tried and tested solutions and a perennial regard for the supremacy of clients' individual requirements. Customers were soon beating a path to Harry Carr's door and emerging delighted, safe in the knowledge that their electrical needs were taken care of. Working relationships established in the company's infancy have withstood the test of time and survive to this day - a testament to Harry's own perspicacity, and the dedication of his highly motivated team.

Projects were varied, and remain so. Over the years, the company has supplied electrical services for customers as diverse as the chemical industry, food manufacturing, hospitals, schools, libraries and power stations. And its home in what has been called 'the Food Town of the North' has led to unrivalled opportunities in an expanding frozen

Above: Harry Carr in 1962.
Below: Harry Carr's Lincolnshire show at Brocklesby Park in 1957.

food industry. Harry Carr Ltd is now justifiably proud of its status as leader in the field of temperature controlled storage and distribution.

Like father like son, the saying goes. Frank Carr joined the company after broad experience elsewhere: university followed by a graduate apprenticeship with Reyrolle and before that two year's service as an electrical officer with the Royal Navy. After five years of Frank joining, Charles Long was also made a director of the company in 1959 and together they steered the company through expansion and development for the next 25 years. They carried on Harry's work, especially

in the refrigeration industry, where the company earned a reputation for being at the forefront of developments in computer control, and to this day is squarely positioned in the vanguard of modern systems and design.

The family tradition continued when Frank's son Michael, a graduate with several years experience in industry, joined the company in 1984. He now heads the organisation as Managing Director and Chairman. Still a family concern, the business demonstrates textbook development: steady progress, unhindered by the vagaries of fad and fashion, a palpable commitment to core principles of service and quality, and an outward-looking management style that is able to capitalise on new ideas and systems. An ongoing training programme ensures that engineers are conversant with design, safety

and technical thinking - up to degree level - but there is a focus too on those starting out: around 30 apprentices are hard at work around the company's three locations (the company's success has allowed expansion from Grimsby to two additional branches in Hull and King's Lynn).

What Harry Carr brought into being in a hut on a Grimsby builder's yard is now a modern, streamlined company, with a workforce of 180, undertaking major design and installation projects, with values of up to £2.5m, throughout the UK. A company with a bright past now blazing a trail to an even brighter future.

Top left: Harry Carr's Certificate of Apprenticeship dates back to 1915.
Top right: Staff christmas dinner in 1956
Left: Harry Carr Limited's premises at West St Mary's Gate.
Below: Current senior management with Frank Carr, from left to right Peter Carr (Works Manager), Michael Carr (Managing Director), Frank Carr and Paddy Richardson (Contracts Director).

Fresh look for Grimsby

Freshney Place shopping centre takes it's name from the River Freshney which runs alongside it. In keeping with a policy to preserve traditional ties with the community, Freshney   Place Centre has retained a number of the original street names on which it is now built and can still be found on old maps of Great Grimsby. These include Baxtergate, Flottergate, Friargate, New Biggin, Clayton Walk, Haven Walk and Brewery Street.

Near to the present location of Friary Walk in the centre was the site of an Augustinian Friary, dating from 1293-1539. Some human remains found there whilst excavating were reburied in Scartho Road Cemetery.

Humberside County Council arranged for two digs to be carried out prior to building works commencing on the proposed extensions to the East and West of the centre. A number of items were found relating back to Saxon times, including leather boots and pottery, details of which can be found in Grimsby Library .

Freshney Place as we know it today, began life with the construction of the Riverhead Centre in 1969. The Riverhead Centre was a typical 1970s shopping precinct, open to the elements. Stores included Guy and Smiths, Lawson and Stockdales both family businesses who now no longer trade in the centre. Locals referred to it as 'the precinct' or 'top town' and it is fondly known by those names today by the older generation in the town. Rows of old, disused terraced houses and properties were demolished for the building of the centre. This was phase one of a three phase building plan which followed some twelve to eighteen months later. Phases one and two terminated where the current Binns and Dolland & Aitchison stores now stand. Phase three was to incorporate the present site of Bhs and Mothercare. Features in it's two main squares included square brick plant containers and benches.

Behind the centre lay Baxtergate roadway and an open-air car park. These two were demolished in the late eighties as Freshney Place was developed to create a new mall now known as Baxergate. A new roadway known as Frederick Ward Way was constructed alongside the River Freshney to replace the old Baxergate road, which is now part of the Freshney Place Shopping Centre Complex. Initially Woolworths formed the Eastern end of the centre but this has also been extended to create more room for additional shops and form an entrance from the bus station.

Freshney Place is bright, airy, fully enclosed centre with glazed, pitched roofing and many decorative features including a water fountain in it's main square and palm trees that also help to create a welcoming shopping environment for its customers. This all provides a luxury setting for over a 100 shop units covering 500,000 square feet of accommodation.

Taking the shape of two parallel malls it has become the retail heart of the town, situated between a new and thriving bus station the highly successful indoor market. Most major multiple retailers are represented in the centre with an excellent range of individual retailers providing a tempting mix for most shoppers.

The Centre has a selection of coffee shops and restaurants, and is serviced by two multi-storey secured car parks offering over 1,000 parking spaces. Parking is competitively priced and the area is clean, light, airy and accessible. This has been recognised by the AA who bestowed their Gold Award on the car parks in 1993 and a further secured car park award in 1998, that is administered by the AA on behalf of the Association of Chief Police Officers, currently the only car park in NE Lincs to hold this award.

Customer care is high priority at Freshney Place, ensuring ease of access for the first time visitor. Well informed and helpful staff are on hand to offer special facilities for the disabled and very young.

The management enjoys a close liaison with the retailers who participate regularly in the Centre's marketing initiatives.

The Centre has close links with other destination areas of Grimsby including the National Fishing Heritage Centre located close to Freshney Place and the new Auditorium.

November 1994 saw the centre launched as a Truancy-Free Zone as a recoginition of the positive Co-operation between the Freshney Place traders, local education authority and the police. Freshney Place is a Hammerson Plc owned property.

Above: A modern aerial view of Freshney Place shopping centre.
Left: The fountain area provides a focal point in the centre.
Facing page: An aerial view from 1988 of the shopping centre.

Chemical reaction

The Cray Valley Plant at Stallingborough on the south bank of the Humber forms part of the resin division of the chemical arm of the French oil and gas company Total. Cray Valley is a leading producer of structural resins used in sanitaryware, boats and vehicles and additives for the coatings industry - paints, inks, varnishes, adhesives and polyester resins and gelcoats for the composites industry.

The origins of the Stallingborough concern lie in a firm established in 1877 by two brothers, George and John William Coates. Their humble business prospered with the rapid growth of the printing industry in the latter part of the 19th century. In 1889 they became a public limited company. Increased revenue led to rapid expansion with new sales outlets in New Zealand, South Africa and India.

By the 1920s the company had established considerable markets overseas and in 1925 marked its technical supremacy with the opening of the first of many laboratories. The following twenty years saw even more rapid expansion and Coates became a public company in 1948. Coates Brothers had become an international organisation, holding a leading position in the world markets for its chosen fields of surface coatings and products for the graphic arts and packaging industries.

Cray Valley had been founded in 1938 to specialise in the development and supply of printing ink resins for its parent company, Coates Brothers.

Established as a joint partnership venture between Laporte Industries and Synres of Holland, the first resins were produced at the Stallingborough complex in 1967. In 1970 the Stallingborough plant was acquired by Coates Brothers to augment the companies capacity for coating resins.

The South Bank site now occupies 17 acres, of which seven are operational. The other ten acres are earmarked for further expansion in the future.

A growth in demand for their product led to a third reactor coming 'on stream' during 1974. Four years later the company stopped making printing ink resins to concentrate on the production of coatings and polyester resins. With sales demand at a high level, further production expansion brought a fourth reactor and associated blenders 'on line'.

Coates Brothers was acquired by the Total Group of Companies in 1990.

Above: A scientist working on new solutions for resin.
Left: An aerial view of Cray Valley's site in Grimsby.

Training is an important company activity and is tailored to meet the needs of the company and the individual. It is applied in the widest sense, through job supervision, internal and external study and practical work, higher education and via challenging projects and assignments. Nearly 50% of all employees are involved in some type of further education. Wherever possible, promotion is from within the company.

Cray Valley is well aware of the strict regulations governing all aspects of environmental protection. By using the skills of highly qualified employees and by introducing more and better technology into production, the company will continue to be one of the world's leading resin manufacturers without damaging the environment. In 1995 a full time environmental specialist was appointed to operate with the inspection agencies on Cray Valley's improvement programme.

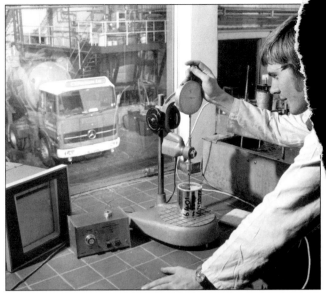

A system for microbiologically treating the effluent was designed, approved and installed during 1995 and the company spent a considerable amount of money to reduce air emissions.

Cray Valley's research programme is focused on developing new products in close co-operation with its customers. The company invests 5% of its turnover each year in research. With its team of scientists of international renown and its very latest equipment, Cray Valley's research centre at Verneuil-en-Halatte in France guarantees excellence and success.

Stallingborough in the UK and Drocourt in France are working to ISO 9002 quality standards. For Polyester Resins Drocourt has been awarded RAQ2 quality rating by the French Ministry of Defence.

Above: A technician keeping an eye on things. Below: From past to present, an example of their modern transport.

tonnes a year of Polycor Iso gelcoats. A full range of them can be colour matched to customers' needs with high quality, non-toxic pigments. They are already extensively used in the UPR industry to give a glossy and resistant finish.

The nineties also brought a concentrated effort to increase efficiency within the plant and make it 'operator-friendly'.

Reorganisation and rationalisation within the Group the following year resulted in the emergence of Cray Valley Limited in January 1992. This was the Resin Division of Total.

In 1993 the filled resin plant came on stream and in the following summer construction began on the Gelcoat Plant. Gelcoats are used with structural resins as a final outside layer on a structure, both for protective and cosmetic reasons. The new unit was commissioned to accommodate an increasing demand for this product line, both in the UK and in other European countries.Cray Valley has built a customer demonstration facility at the Stallingborough site which is used especially to demonstrate applications of the new gelcoat technology to customers and potential customers under optimum conditions. Clear white brush or spray gelcoats have been manufactured at Stallingborough for more than 20 years but the new automated gelcoat plant has the capacity to produce 3,000

Cray Valley now has a workforce of around 100 and the company insists that its progress and development is due to the willing co-operation of all of them. The management believes in the recruitment, motivation and retention of the highest calibre staff in every role from factory floor to board level.

Above: An operator drumming off in the polyester building.
Below: A celebration of faces past and present.